TO IAIN

With best wishes,

Alan H

# CRICKET·CONJUROR

A slow left-armer
And quite a charmer,
Johnny Wardle
Didn't dawdle,
Though they don't play
He bowled chinamen,
And on his day
He'd clown away;
A drive, waist high
Past him would fly
Like a rocket
To the boundary,
He'd turn, look that way,
But the ball was pouched –
Safely in his pocket.

**Colin Shakespeare**
'Seamers' (Oak Press 1983)

# Johnny Wardle
# CRICKET · CONJUROR

## Alan Hill

**David & Charles**
Newton Abbot  London  North Pomfret (Vt)

To all my old friends in South
Yorkshire who helped to polish
my talents as a writer.

© Alan Hill 1988
© Statistics Roy Wilkinson 1988
© Line Drawings John Wardle

**British Library Cataloguing in Publication Data**
Hill, Alan. 1928–
  Cricket conjuror.
  1. Wardle, Johnny  2. Cricket players –
  England – Biography
  I. Title
  796.35'8'0924          GV915.W/

ISBN 0-7153-9053-3

All rights reserved. No part of this
publication may be reproduced, stored
in a retrieval system, or transmitted,
in any form or by any means, electronic,
mechanical, photocopying, recording or
otherwise, without the prior permission
of David & Charles Publishers plc

Photoset by Northern Phototypesetting Co, Bolton
and printed in Great Britain
by Billings & Sons Ltd, Worcester
for David & Charles Publishers plc
Brunel House, Newton Abbot, Devon

# Contents

| | | |
|---|---|---|
| | Foreword | 6 |
| | Introduction | 8 |
| 1 | Aggression and Artistry | 12 |
| 2 | A Fine Romance | 20 |
| 3 | The Marathon Man | 26 |
| 4 | Alliance with Appleyard | 41 |
| 5 | Locked in a Masquerade | 53 |
| 6 | Havoc at Manchester | 74 |
| 7 | A Winning Message at Cape Town | 91 |
| 8 | Furious Departure | 105 |
| 9 | Burnet on Wardle | 116 |
| 10 | A Friendly Cage for a Lion | 122 |
| 11 | The Happy Cricketer | 139 |
| 12 | Visions in Retirement | 148 |
| | Statistical Appendices | 158 |
| | Index | 167 |

# Foreword
by Norman Yardley,
the former Yorkshire and England captain

ALAN HILL has, I hope, done something to rekindle the interest in the sadly dying art of spin bowling. His two excellent books, *A Chain of Spin Wizards* (the story of Yorkshire's famed left-arm tradition) and the award-winning biography of Hedley Verity are now being followed by one on that great character, Johnny Wardle.

Many will fondly remember Johnny most for his humorous antics and his entertaining batting – particularly at his beloved Bramall Lane, his home ground at Sheffield. But it would be unwise to lay too much stress on the fun. Make no mistake, behind this facade Johnny was a true, knowledgeable and dedicated professional. In my tribute to him in the *Yorkshire Year Book* I wrote: 'What captain could have wished more than having Johnny Wardle in his side. Whatever the conditions you knew that when you threw him the ball he would do a thoroughly professional job.'

Unfortunately his career did not end on a happy note. He was dismissed by Yorkshire and his own articles in the national press resulted in the withdrawal by the MCC of the invitation to tour Australia in 1958–9. This was a tragedy because he was a greater bowler when this happened than at any time during his career. He was an orthodox left-arm spinner of the highest class and he had, in addition, perfected the art of the chinaman and googly. As a wrist-spinner he compared favourably with two other great 'back-of-the-hand' bowlers, George Tribe and Jack Walsh. He was, in fact, a genius.

Happily, in the long term, all was forgiven and harmony prevailed. Johnny was elected an Honorary Life Member of Yorkshire and he was a welcome guest at Headingley. He was respected as a wise counsellor and put a great deal back into the game, coaching and passing on his expertise at all levels. Before his sad death he had agreed to assist with the coaching of the Yorkshire bowlers. It was a matter of great regret that his illness prevented him from taking up the post.

Johnny will be remembered with affection for all the pleasure he gave throughout the cricketing world. His entertainment value was enormous.

# Introduction

JOHNNY WARDLE, like a modern Don Quixote, flourished his defiant lance in a field of windmills. But unlike Cervantes' chivalrous knight, the 'menacing giants' upon which he severed his spear were a real threat and not the creatures of a fantasy.

Reconciling the contradictions of Wardle's personality has been a formidable task. For those people who did not gain his trust he appeared to have enough chips on his shoulders to build a bonfire. There was a strain of eccentricity in his nature. In his happier moments he was a brilliant comic, who quietly revelled in astonishing fellow players and spectators with his buffoonery.

Johnny once said that his flights of fun were really employed to relieve his own tension. In the Lancashire League, where he found an hospitable harbour for his talents, the popular 'clown prince' image is regarded as superficial. 'If he could get a laugh or two en route that was all right by him. But what he was really there for was to win,' says one cricket associate of those days. Yet Johnny's jokes established him as a character as endearing as any in the history of the game. He was idolised because he could move crowds to admiration as well as laughter.

The humour which gained him the accolade of a great entertainer – quite the best in the view of many contemporaries – might also have masked his distress at the lack of appreciation of his talents. Wardle was a proud man and was aggrieved at the disdain of his critics. The rebellious, unpredictable side of his character surfaced because he was devalued as a bowler and as the heir to Hedley Verity and Wilfred Rhodes. He was an embattled cricketer who was constantly having to prove himself with Yorkshire and England. As a reflection on his beleaguered state, Johnny said: 'A lot of players, a hell of a lot, thought I couldn't bowl. They were amazed when they were having a cigarette, and I'd done them again.'

I have listened respectfully to the protestations of the Yorkshire elders that Wardle was not inhibited from parading his versatility as a bowler. It is, however, my conclusion that his uncommon skills as a wrist-spinner were used too sparingly. Yorkshire, tied to their illustrious orthodox left-arm tradition, could not accept that Johnny had other equally valuable gifts at his command.

In the circumstances, one marvels at his resolution in shouldering an enormous burden in his early years with Yorkshire, and taking over 1,800 first-class wickets during a career which ended on a predictably controversial note. Johnny and his wife, Edna, devoted and resilient partners, showed the same resolution in overcoming seemingly insurmountable handicaps to prosper in their later business venture.

Johnny Wardle, as this book demonstrates, was a master craftsman and a dedicated Yorkshireman who wore his White Rose with pride. He was as singleminded in his pursuit of perfection as any of his renowned predecessors in the county lists. Like them, he was rigorous, even ruthless, in his approach to cricket, and rightly intolerant of those who did not observe the highest standards of conduct on and off the field. No one, not even his worst enemy, challenged his integrity; but the price he paid for his often unnerving honesty was his abrupt dismissal from the Yorkshire ranks in 1958.

Along with Yorkshire and England contemporaries, I believe that his departure was a great loss to the English game. Wiser counsels should have prevailed to avoid this extreme measure which, in the words of Wardle's old bowling partner, Bob Appleyard, was to have immense repercussions for Yorkshire cricket.

Wardle escaped his Yorkshire travail to find contentment in Lancashire League cricket with Nelson and Rishton and with Cambridgeshire in the Minor Counties championship. There was comfort, too, in his belated reconciliation with Yorkshire and his appointment as the county's bowling consultant shortly before his death in 1985. Mike Cowan, in his funeral address, echoed the thoughts of younger Yorkshire players like Geoff Cope, one beneficiary of Wardle's wisdom:

> Johnny was always at his happiest when any young player approached him for advice. To hear him advise, correct a weakness, and relate his experiences, was an education experienced by a fortunate few. It was an untapped source of cricketing knowledge. But those who heard would never forget.

Godfrey Evans has said that Wardle's good points far outweighed his bad ones. One of the most telling examples of the generosity of a misunderstood man came in a recent letter from a Wolverhampton resident. As a collector of cricket first-day cover envelopes, he wrote to Johnny to ask for his signature. This was duly provided but the envelope was later lost. My correspondent sent another envelope, explaining what had happened, and he was rewarded with a magnificent response. From his own collection Johnny sent him an envelope commemorating the centenary of England-Australia Tests in 1977. It contained more than 30 autographs of the cricket celebrities whom Wardle had met in Melbourne. 'I thought this was fantastic and showed the character of a man, much maligned by some people, who was prepared to make a gesture like that.'

The remembrances of a great cricketer have been tinged with affection, respect and regret in many conversations and correspondence with Johnny's legion of friends. I am, of course, especially grateful to the Wardle family (Edna, John and Gerald) for their support and for placing a wealth of material at my disposal; and to Norman Yardley, Wardle's former Yorkshire captain, for kindly supplying the foreword to the book.

In South Yorkshire Mick Pope has carried out invaluable research on Wardle's early days in local league cricket. This has been supplemented by the recollections of former Denaby secretary, John Humphries, and close friends, Ellis and Basil Robinson, Charlie Lee, Henry Walters, Jack Sokell and Charlie Heaton. I must also acknowledge the courteous assistance of the British Newspaper Library staff at Colindale, London; and Guy Williams (Yorkshire Television), Don Rowan and Tony Bradbury (Yorkshire CCC Southern Group) for their support and encouragement during the project.

I am also greatly indebted to the late Bill Bowes, Sir Leonard Hutton, Ted Lester, Bob Appleyard, Bill Sutcliffe, Brian Close, Geoff Cope, Roy Booth, Bob Platt, Ray Illingworth, Mike Cowan, Don Wilson, Tony Woodhouse and Sid Fielden for their memories which have helped me to tease out the true nature Wardle. Ronnie Burnet has also delivered his views on the Yorkshire controversy of 1958 and expressed his sadness at the events which led to Wardle's dismissal.

In Lancashire my allies have been Jim Clarke, the Lancashire League secretary; Alan Haigh and Neville Wood (Nelson) and Bernard Hurst and David Lomas (Rishton). All have paid handsome tribute to the professionalism and guidance of their Yorkshire guest. Maurice Crouch and David Farnell in Cambridgeshire and Wardle's friends and team-mates at his last cricket port of call, the South Yorkshire village club of Barnby Dun, have also joined in the chorus of praise.

## Introduction

Finally, it has been salutary to listen to eminent judges outside Yorkshire. Peter May, Godfrey Evans, Trevor Bailey, Sir George ('Gubby') Allen, Roy Tattersall, Frank Tyson, Keith Andrew, Doug Insole, Freddie Brown, Jim Swanton, Russell Endean and Arthur Morris all rejoice in their memories of a grand sportsman. A champion assembly has hailed a champion cricketer.

Contemporary newspaper reports in the *Yorkshire Post* and *Yorkshire Evening Post*; the Sheffield *Star*, the *South Yorkshire Times*; the *Cape Times* and *Natal Mercury* in South Africa; and various editions of *Wisden Cricketers' Almanack* have provided the nucleus of the printed sources in the book. Permission has been received to quote extracts from the following books:

Alex Bannister, *Cricket Cauldron* (Stanley Paul, 1954); Colin Cowdrey, *MCC – Autobiography of a Cricketer* (Hodder and Stoughton, 1976); Jim Laker, *Spinning Round the World* and *Over to Me* (Frederick Muller, 1957 and 1960); Peter May, *A Game Enjoyed* (Stanley Paul, 1985); Ian Peebles, *The Ashes, 1954–5* (Hodder and Stoughton, 1955); Alan Ross, *Cape Summer* (Hamish Hamilton, 1957); E. W. Swanton, *West Indian Adventure* (Museum Press, 1954), *Report from South Africa – with P.B.H. May's MCC Team, 1956–57* (Robert Hale, 1957); Len Hutton, *Just My Story* (Hutchinson, 1956).

Other books consulted were: John Arlott, *Test Match Diary, 1953* (James Barrie, 1953), *Australian Test Journal* (Phoenix Books, 1955); *Days at the Cricket* (Longmans Green, 1950); Brian Close, *I Don't Bruise Easily* (Macdonald and Janes, 1978); Sir Donald Bradman, *Farewell to Cricket* (Hodder and Stoughton, 1953); Norman Cutler, *Behind the South African Tests* (Putnam, 1955); Charles Fortune, *The MCC Tour of South Africa, 1956–57* (George G. Harrap, 1957); Tony Lock, *For Surrey and England*, (Hodder and Stoughton, 1957); David Lemmon, Editor, *Cricket Heroes* (Queen Anne Press, 1984); John Kay, *Cricket in the Leagues*, (Eyre and Spottiswoode, 1970); Gordon Ross, *Surrey* (Arthur Barker, 1971); Roy McLean, *Pitch and Toss* (Hodder and Stoughton, 1957); Ray Robinson, *The Glad Season*, (Collins, 1955); A. A. Thomson, *Cricket My Happiness* (Museum Press, 1954); J. H. Wardle, *Happy go Johnny* (Robert Hale, 1957).

Alan Hill,
Lindfield, Sussex
*September, 1987*

# 1
# Aggression and Artistry

*'This little bugger will play for Yorkshire'* – South Yorkshire cricket captain.

THE chameleon nature of cricket folk hero Johnny Wardle could charm and offend, by turn, even his most loyal friends. He was a man capable of enormous generosity to those who gained his trust. As a stern perfectionist, he was equally incapable of compromise; in matters which could be accounted trivial, and yet for him carried the slur of cheating, he was merciless in his anger.

Wardle's fiercely competitive spirit brought him pleasure and pain. He was, as many people have said, eccentric and often irritating as he swung between the poles of two characters – one happy and carefree and the other bitter and obstinate. One South Yorkshireman who knew Wardle from his boyhood days comments:

> I could always see that Johnny was going to make foes because he was an inflexible man. I don't think he saw any of his own warts. The fact that very few people got close to him meant that his good points, and these were considerable, did not often get an airing.

Betraying Wardle's outward belligerence was the sensitivity of an artist which shone through his nimble fingers on a rich cricket canvas. The stirring of the colours of a bewitching art began in the sporting stronghold of South Yorkshire. The area was a treasure trove of talent, boasting England soccer and cricket players; three of the Manchester United stars killed in the Munich air disaster; and among the competitive girls, one Olympics sprinter. Johnny Wardle would later fit easily and handsomely into this celebrity category.

Surprisingly, in these circumstances, Wardle could not call upon the inspiration of a family cricket background; but his parents, Jack and Jane Wardle, must have speedily acknowledged the symptoms and succumbed to his fanaticism while he was still a child. 'I had a flat bat and a ball when I was only three,' said Johnny. 'I was a natural, just crackers about the game, and cricket must have been born in me. I always had a ball in my hand, an apple or an orange would do, and I would spin it from finger to finger.'

Wardle, one of three children, was born at Ardsley, near Barnsley on 8 January 1923. At the age of four he moved with his family to the neighbouring village of Brampton. His new home in the mining terrace of Cliffe Road overlooked the colliery cricket ground. To spend his childhood beside the field and within a comfortable six-hit of his bedroom window must have seemed to the young Johnny a kind of paradise.

One of Wardle's boyhood friends, who lingered happily at his side in the alleys and lanes of the village, was the Barnsley footballer, Henry Walters. They played together as children and later became workmates at Cortonwood Colliery. Walters recalls:

> Johnny was always a big lad with a pair of shoulders more befitting a fast bowler. There would be about eight of us who knocked about as a regular gang. Johnny was the oldest and the strongest. Even from a very early age he had tremendous potential as a cricketer. He was always a cut above us and we thought we were pretty decent.

Walters adds: 'But that didn't stop us from knocking his bowling about or bowling him out cheaply. That didn't go down too well, and since he invariably supplied the tackle for our little games, the matches could end abruptly if he finished on the losing side.' The eccentric side of Johnny's character also surfaces in Walters' remembrances of his companion. 'You dare not cross his path. He was a prankster as well and you never knew whether he was joking or serious. I would do anything for him, but it was difficult to get close to him because his moods changed so quickly.'

The clatter of the composition balls against tar barrels in the Brampton lanes faded as the boys grew older. The adjoining cricket field had a magnetic attraction. They hung around the village ground in the hope of receiving twopence for putting up the scoreboard tins. They revelled in the privilege of fielding out on first eleven practice nights, and helped to pull the heavy roller up and down the wicket. 'We were never out of the field,' says Walters. 'As long as we were involved in the cricket, no matter how menial the task, we were grateful.'

As a boy at Brampton Ellis School, Johnny hit the first of the spectacular sixes which were to become his trademark in first-class cricket. He won a scholarship to Wath-on-Dearne Grammar School at the age of eleven. Three years later in the House Cup final he took eight wickets for four runs, a feat which earned him the prize of a bat autographed by one of his Yorkshire and England heroes, Herbert Sutcliffe. The achievement did not ruffle his lordly school seniors, who considered him much too young or too junior to play or even practise with them.

Johnny's response was to seek opportunities elsewhere, and at the end of the school day he made his way to the Brampton ground. He was always ready to bowl to the big men, or to fill a last-minute vacancy as number eleven. The reward for his persistence was a place in the South Yorkshire League side, or the team playing in the Mexborough Evening League. Wardle delighted in telling the story of his entry into the exalted circle of the school first eleven. One of his matches for Brampton was against the vaunted Hickleton Main Colliery team. In the opposing ranks was the Wath School captain. Johnny took three wickets for 14 runs and found immense pleasure in shattering the stumps of the school cricket elder. There was an immediate gain in stature and status. By the following season Wardle was installed as a member of the school first eleven and topped the batting and bowling averages.

The school prizegiving at the end of the term produced a sickening blow to Johnny's pride. Four caps were duly awarded and he was halfway out of his seat when he realised, to his horror, that the remaining one was to be presented to someone else. It was the first of his disappointments in cricket. Johnny had worn his Yorkshire cap for almost ten years and collected a score of England caps before the school remedied what must surely have been an oversight. In 1956, he attended a reunion dinner of the Old Wathonians and was belatedly presented with his school cap and colours.

Wardle's formative years in Yorkshire Council cricket were played against the sombre backcloth of approaching war. He bounced confidently on the springboard of youthful success. The ominous events in Europe overshadowed his sporting dreams. Before the outbreak of war financial support was offered by one member of the family for him to continue his education. Despite the pleadings of this benefactor and his headmaster, Johnny chose to leave school and take a job as an apprentice fitter at Hickleton Main Colliery. The working hours dovetailed neatly with time for cricket, so Johnny was able to justify his decision, at least to his own satisfaction.

Cricket always ranked first in Johnny's sporting priorities. Lower down the scale were his other accomplishments as a rugby full-back (at Wath Grammar School) and afterwards in soccer as a skilful left-winger and feared penalty marksman. His adroit footwork as a footballer was to be exploited later on the cricket field. His juggling tricks with feet and hands were performed with the high glee of a circus clown. Wardle flirted briefly with professional football, attracting the attention of the Wolverhampton Wanderers' scout in South Yorkshire, Mark Crook. But his lack of pace as a winger meant that he was never likely to offer a serious challenge to other touchline masters who thrilled the post-war crowds at Molineux.

Johnny was a member, along with Henry Walters, of the Wolves nursery team, Wath Wanderers. Major Frank Buckley, the famed manager of Wolves, paid him the compliment of inviting him for trials. Johnny played in wartime regional football with the Midlands club before a knee injury threatened his cricket aspirations. His soccer campaigns, as Walters observes, bristled with the determination he applied to cricket. The keenness sometimes overstepped the bounds of caution, as in one match between Wath Wanderers and a strong RASC team at Sheffield.

The army eleven included several league players, and they were defending an unbeaten record extending over many months. It was a rugged game of fluctuating fortunes. The match ended in a 4–4 draw after Wath had taken the lead at one stage. Johnny, provoking or provoked, was the victim of a heavy tackle. He sprang to his feet to land a punch on his rival and was sent off by the referee.

Wardle's cricket forays were spiced with equal vigour on the tiny Brampton field. One contemporary wryly remarks: 'six leg byes were not uncommon.' At fifteen, while still a schoolboy, Johnny was already giving a foretaste of his all-round potential. He scored his first half-century in a partnership with his captain, Sid Ellis, against Ackworth. His reward was a collection of six shillings and eightpence. 'Wardle attacked the bowling in great style,' ran a report in the *South Yorkshire Times*. 'His defence was extremely good. He timed his shots admirably and invariably gave the fielders no chance with clean hits over the boundary rails.'

The plaudits insistently dwelt on his bowling merits as Johnny gathered in his harvest of wickets. One of his early exploits for Hickleton Main was against Thorncliffe. He secured 7 wickets for 26 runs in nine overs in a match-winning spell. In four out of five seasons he won the Yorkshire Council's junior bowling prize, with returns of between 30 and 45 wickets and steadily improving averages. 'It got to a stage where Johnny was almost unplayable,' says another South Yorkshire friend. 'He would bowl them out as fast as they came in.' Wardle did not suffer the frustrations of today's fledgling spinners. 'This is where I was lucky as a kid; the captain of the local club fancied me. I was only 15, but I got plenty of bowling. He used to say: "This little bugger will play for Yorkshire".'

In 1940, the 17-year-old Wardle, after one season at Hickleton, returned to Brampton to achieve the resounding feat of all ten wickets in an innings against Rockingham. 'To Wardle, of Brampton, has fallen the felicity of being the first bowler in local cricket to take all 10 wickets this season,' reported the *South Yorkshire Times*. 'In 17 overs against Rockingham he bowled five maidens and dismissed all 10 batsmen for 36 runs.' Johnny, or Jack, as he was often called, was rapidly earning the accolade of a phenomenon. In August he announced his authority as a batsman, hitting with typical fury to reach a century over local rivals, Mexborough. Johnny was unbeaten with 104 (out of 263) as Brampton won by 77 runs.

Wardle's early cricket mentors included Colin Kilner, the younger brother of Roy, the Yorkshire and England all-rounder. Kilner, who played for the Mitchell Main Colliery Club, once asked Johnny how he bowled his quicker ball. He was dissatisfied with the youngster's wavering reply and proceeded to explain how to hold the ball with the seam up so that it would swing. This quicker ball, as Johnny began to devote himself to the principles of spin, was sparingly employed. It was a surprise weapon in his armoury. So was his chinaman (the left-hander's off-break) and googly, then at an experimental stage of practice.

Johnny's faster ball and his teasing wrist-spinners were to become linked to the variations of his more commonly used orthodox finger spin in his first-class bowling repertoire. In local cricket, and at times with Yorkshire, he occasionally opened with the new ball, perhaps to enable him to loosen up before reverting to his normal form of attack. Charlie Lee, a fellow South Yorkshireman who played for Yorkshire and Derbyshire, remembers Johnny's 'steady little inducers' and how they were pitched with splendid accuracy.

Lee provides another memory of Johnny's stature in local cricket at Brampton and the response of a rival left-arm bowler, Frank Ellis, of Swinton. 'Frank was a little envious of Johnny, who was even then considered a Yorkshire prospect.' In one match Swinton ran up a total of 260 for the loss of only two wickets. Wardle had one of his less happy days as a bowler, conceding nearly 100 runs. Ellis said: 'He can't bowl. Look at his figures.' When Brampton batted Johnny wreaked awful vengeance on his challenger. As they walked off the field, one Swinton player turned to Ellis and remarked: 'Well, you said he couldn't bowl. I'll tell you this, he can bloody well bat.'

Another story concerns the baffling enticements of Wardle's chinaman, which Henry Walters considers was his friend's stock-in-trade and an under-used asset. As in later years, Johnny mostly relied on orthodox spin to outwit the early order batsmen. This was often a prelude to a demoralising, instructive display of wrist-spin.

In one local knock-out competition at Shaw Lane, Barnsley, the opponents were Worsborough Bridge. Wardle's last victim was wicket-keeper Bill Lilley, of Mitchell Main. 'Now Johnny and Bill were good pals,' relates Walters. 'They'd got to know each other because Johnny was doing his courting down in Bill's village. Bill was a good stumper, but he weren't too handy with the bat.' Walters remembers that he was fielding behind Wardle at mid-on.

> Johnny moved in and bowled his chinaman. He threw it right up and well out. And while it was still in the air he took his cap and sweater from the umpire and began to walk towards the pavilion. Bill was bowled neck and crop. Johnny, cheeky lad, knew what would happen as soon as the ball left his hand.

As the drive for victory on the European battlefront raged fiercely, Wardle was winning his own campaign for county recognition at home in South Yorkshire. In 1942 he attended a Yorkshire coaching session at Barnsley. His tutor was the buoyant George Hirst, a man of infectious friendliness, who could lift the spirits of even the most fumbling novice. Hirst said of his pupils: 'Several of them are really promising cricketers in the all-round sense. Among those who shaped particularly well was J. H. Wardle, the Brampton all-rounder.'

One Wath-on-Dearne man was an attentive patrol in the covers, his eyes raised upwards as the catches beckoned from steepling hits, during Wardle's record season at Denaby in 1944. Johnny's tally of 113 wickets at 7.85 runs each broke the previous Yorkshire Council record held by Ellis Robinson, the Yorkshire off-spinner with whom he was to bowl in post-war county cricket. Charlie Heaton was a key fielding ally at Denaby. He remembers Wardle's expertise as a slow bowler at Tickhill Square where the wicket gleamed like a newly varnished table and permitted no easy conquests.

Quite early in his record season Wardle had given abundant warning that he would scale imposing heights. Against his old club, Brampton, he took 8 wickets for 30 runs; in a low-scoring game at Rotherham, on a soft wicket tailored for his spin, he collected 6 wickets to bowl out the home side for 51; and against Sheffield

United at Bramall Lane he added another 7 wickets to the lengthening list. As the wickets tumbled, Wardle did not neglect his batting opportunities. At Rockingham where he had revelled in his 10 wickets' triumph four years earlier, his power was bewildering. He struck 32 in seven hits, including five sixes. He also took 8 wickets as Denaby won by three wickets.

By late August Wardle had secured his 100th wicket. In a dominating finale to a season of swift dispatches he took 12 wickets, six each in games against Elsecar and Wath, to pass the record milestone. It sealed his arrival as a bowler of glittering promise.

Wardle's ascent towards county status won him a massive following at Denaby and throughout South Yorkshire. Opponents always looked, with some trepidation, to see if his name was on the team sheet. His reputation as a bowler and hard-hitting batsman induced a devout awe. 'Johnny was always a good team man, keen to win, and ever ready to help on and off the field,' says another long-standing friend. 'He was so excited and proud of his achievements.'

The inspirational qualities of Wardle are remembered by former Denaby secretary, John Humphries. Along with other mining folk he would put aside more mundane tasks to join in the chorus of praise. In the pre-war years Denaby, unlike their popular football neighbours at Tickhill Square, had not succeeded in generating spectator interest. Good players, mostly imported to work at the collieries (Ellis Robinson's family came to the area from Cumbria), excellent subsidised facilities, and many fine performances on the field elicited a dismal response at the turnstiles.

The signing of Kilner Bateson, a charismatic figure as captain, from Conisbrough in the Doncaster League was the signal for a revival in the club's fortunes. Bateson recruited two fast bowlers, George Porter and Charlie Pegg. The newcomers were to harness their speed to Wardle's spin and prove a formidable combination at Tickhill Square. Bateson played an important part in Wardle's development as a cricketer in his four seasons at Denaby. John Humphries recalls:

> Killie took particular care to integrate John with the rest of the team. He got a good response from his protégé, pulled the best out of him, fitting him into the side as a club man. John was fortunate to have such a fine captain.

Humphries also remembers Wardle's exceptional accuracy as a wrist-spinner and how earnestly he sought control over his chinamen and googlies at the twice-weekly practice sessions at Denaby.

Wicket-keeper George Allen, known inevitably as 'Nudger' and recruited from the Nottingham area, was Johnny's adviser in his quest for all-round spin. Allen was renowned in South Yorkshire cricket circles for his agility behind the stumps. 'He influenced John greatly with his knowledge about opposing batsmen, and in his timing in the use of wrist-spin. John appreciated this help and they were a great combination,' says Humphries.

In one game at Rockingham Wardle was brought into the attack at the fall of the third wicket.

> He had little success at the outset and the score had reached the middle nineties. John then took the fourth wicket with a big off-break and then, with identical balls, he took the next six wickets inside two more overs. Rockingham did not reach three figures. It was a remarkable performance.

Humphries says Wardle was an esteemed player, popular with teammates and opponents alike. 'He never forgot his friends at Denaby where, in the dark days of the war, he had found such a welcome stage for his great ability.' It is a compliment which is echoed by many other South Yorkshire contemporaries. Wardle did not turn his back on those who had befriended him and fostered his talents.

Johnny was perhaps at his happiest amid the bonhomie of the solid, forthright pitmen. His heart beat steadily with them. Bob Platt, a later Yorkshire colleague, now says: 'I wish I could have run my life with the same degree of honesty and the professional way in which Johnny applied himself to the game of cricket.' Wardle's lifestyle was forged in the tightly-knit community of South Yorkshire. It excluded shallow dealings and polite pretence. He possessed the defects as well as the virtues of the truly honest man.

# 2
# A Fine Romance

*'Johnny was my anchor; he always seemed in charge of his life' – Edna Wardle.*

THE Sunday evening parade in Wombwell Park brought together the boys and girls of the village in a swaggering ritual of courtship. For the young Edna Howson, a sporting champion in her own right as a local swimmer and runner, this was just a promenade before bedtime. She was content with the thought that her absent boyfriend, Roy Cooling, a Yorkshire schools' cricketer, had no peer in this company.

As she made her farewells, one young man seemed anxious to delay her departure. He walked patiently by her side, quite determined to advance his claims for her affections. Edna recalls: 'I told him that my boy Roy was a far better cricketer than he was.' Johnny Wardle, as the persistent suitor, delivered his winning rejoinder. 'Well,' he told her with some relish, 'I scored a century yesterday.'

The lustre of Roy was rather dimmed by this revelation. He was rapidly eclipsed by Johnny whose growing success as a cricketer won the approval of his future father-in-law, Cyril Howson. He was proud that Edna had such a grand young man. Edna and Johnny next met at Wombwell Feast. 'He impressed me greatly by knocking all the coconuts down. My arms were full of prizes. I thought he was great.' It was the start of a romance, buffeted here and there by Johnny's frenzy in tiffs with the capricious Edna, but kept intact by an enduring devotion. They were married at Wombwell Parish Church in April 1943.

Their first married home was a little 'two up and two down' house in Princess Street, West Melton. This was where Edna and her neighbours, Mollie and Lily, each of them with two frolicking boys, clung to a precarious living in those days of wartime austerity. Johnny had to maintain a commendable sense of humour to keep pace with his madcap young wife. One friend said: 'It must be nice being married to Edna.' Johnny replied 'Yes, it is, but it can be frightening at times.' Edna lived in a torment of uncertainty. She was caught up in a series of cliffhanger situations. That she survived them was a source of relief and also of astonishment. She was so accident-prone that the Wardles likened her to Lucille Ball, the American film comedienne, who displayed similar hapless tendencies on the screen.

Edna's saving graces were her vivaciousness, her thrift as a penny-wise housewife, and her unswerving loyalty to Johnny in all situations. She was also rare among cricket wives as a confidante. Johnny found it easier to discuss his problems with her than with his Yorkshire team-mates. They formed a resilient partnership.

Johnny played the incorrigible droll as he ragged his zany, delightful Edna. His tricks often reduced the family to helpless laughter. There was the incident of the sweets when Edna and her friend Lily took a respite from their household chores to enjoy a shilling's-worth of escapism at the local cinema. On one outing Edna was perplexed by her sweet, which was quite lacking in flavour. When the lights went up she took it out from beneath her blackened tongue to discover that it was a small piece of coal. Johnny had unwrapped and discarded the proper sweets bought at the corner shop. He had substituted cubes of coal and concealed them tightly in the bag.

The Wardles, like most of their friends, dipped into their meagre budget to pay for the Christmas drinks, the bottles of sherry and port, on a club instalments plan. Edna recalls another of Johnny's pranks. It was a bitterly cold winter and she was upstairs cleaning the bedrooms. The Christmas Club bottle of sherry was stored in a wardrobe. She decided she would have a little drink to fortify herself against the cold. Relaxing by the side of the bed, she took a sip from the glass. The sherry was sour, it was clearly an inferior brand. When Johnny returned home from his work at the colliery she told him, with some indignation, that she was taking the sherry back to the shop. 'I put my coat on, tucked the bottle under my arm, and turned to find Johnny with a broad grin on his face. He had decanted the sherry into a lemonade bottle and filled the other bottle with vinegar and water.'

On another winter's day Johnny had been working overtime and returned home for a late lunch. Snow was heaped high in the outside yard as Edna, her apron flapping in the draught, prepared the

Yorkshire pudding in her small kitchen. She mopped her brow as if in a heat-wave and was completely oblivious to the icy blasts sweeping through the open door into the room.

'Keep that door open,' she commanded Johnny in her most imperious manner. He protested but obeyed the order. 'I turned round to serve his meal and there was Johnny with a solemn face. He was sitting at the table, with his cap, scarf and coat on, holding his knife and fork, and waiting for his pudding.' Honours were declared even in this little family jest.

The affair of the de-luxe wireless which cost £28 – a lot of money in the early years of their marriage – sorely offended Edna's sense of thrift.

> I was furious with Johnny for buying it. We hadn't got a dining chair or a carpet. It seemed an awful waste. Music did not mean much to me, but it did to Johnny. I thought it was dreadful to spend so much money when we had hardly any furniture and certainly nothing comfortable to sit on so that we could enjoy the music.

Essentially, though, Johnny usually made the right decisions, however impulsive or misguided they might have seemed to Edna at times. The humorist was at heart a serious man, never soft or silly. 'Johnny was my anchor; he always seemed in charge of his life,' says Edna. 'He was a perfectionist and his tolerance did have short limits. Suddenly, if you couldn't see what he was trying to explain, he would explode.' Edna laughed at her recollections of her husband. 'But you have to know dizzy me to understand Johnny's reaction.'

Johnny's eldest son, John, believes that his father's adult personality was probably influenced by the unchallenged power of his grandmother.

> She was a small, wiry woman, the driving force and the boss in the house. It suited grandad, who was a quiet, easy-going chap and enjoyed his game of bowls and a pint of beer at the local working men's club. Dad, on the other hand, disliked domineering women. Mum had to play a more gentle role, using her wiles to get what she wanted.

The hard self-sufficiency, which was to sustain the Wardles in times of cricket adversity, was coupled with an enterprise which enabled them to escape the mean, companionable streets of West Melton and move into semi-detached suburbia in Wakefield. Johnny's fame as a cricketer undoubtedly provided the spur and the means for the move. But it also afforded him a privacy which he considered of paramount importance in his family life. Whenever possible, he commuted home from cricket matches.

As a young Yorkshire cricketer, he once astonished his neighbours at West Melton by arriving home by taxi with a heavyweight cargo of cricket bags. The responsibility of transporting the team tackle from match to match was entrusted to county juniors by the Yorkshire captain, Brian Sellers. Johnny was the bagman in this season. He had worked out the timetable so that he could have a break with Edna and the boys. On the following evening another cab was called to transfer the bagman and the mountain of equipment to the railway station for the journey to London and Yorkshire's next game.

This enterprising interlude demonstrated the importance of his home for Johnny. In these surroundings the highs and lows of his career could be placed in proper perspective. He coveted his later status as an England cricketer, but the months of touring, pulling him apart from his beloved Edna, were the severest of trials. The contents of their letters, which flew to and fro across the world, spill over with expressions of heartache and loneliness. Across the miles both Edna and Johnny were ticking off the days until his return. 'It is fantastic to think that at least two people in our generation have got the right partner,' wrote Johnny during one cricket tour. 'Mum was Dad's world outside cricket,' says the Wardles' younger son, Gerald.

Gerald's remembrances of his father are of an unassuming man, who did not carry the aura of an international sportsman. 'My friends – and some of them were rough 'uns – never got kicked out. It was always open house, as long as we behaved ourselves.'

Johnny encouraged his sons to play all sports. There were snooker and table tennis tables at their Wakefield home. In his games with Gerald and John the elder Wardle made few if any concessions. 'In the early days we were learning, but as we improved in ability Dad would try to stop us winning,' says Gerald. 'He might let you get close to him, but he wouldn't give you a game. He never threw anything.'

Gerald, a talented wicket-keeper as a teenager, always played sport for fun in contrast to his brother John who shared his father's intense competitiveness. John Wardle was to become a fine club cricketer, playing as a slow left-arm bowler for London University and Forest Hill in the South Thames League in the late 1960s and 1970s. In 1975 he took 122 wickets at 10.5 runs each and scored over 800 runs for Forest Hill. He was also a member of the Club Cricket Conference party which toured Australia.

Edna Wardle says: 'If you could have combined Gerald's talent with John's enthusiasm you might have got another Johnny. Gerald decided that he would never be as good as his Dad and was not prepared to compete.' Gerald's rapidly waning enthusiasm enraged his brother during their games of cricket as boys. 'I always wanted to bat. When it was my turn to bowl I would go and play cowboys and Indians. John was furious,' recalls Gerald.

Detecting signs of their father's displeasure ws as difficult for the Wardle boys as it was for Johnny's county cricket colleagues. 'Dad was certainly unpredictable, or so it seemed to me as a child,' says Gerald. 'In minor offences he would hit the roof, serious misdemeanours he would take in his stride.' He remembers the time when the family moved to Thorne, near Doncaster to start a business, which was later to become a thriving social club. One important item was an old van, which was used to gather weeds and dump them. 'John and I, then aged about 15 or 16, used to love getting into the van and driving it.'

On one of their skylarking trips John was at the wheel of the van when it careered into a pond on the site. 'John and I were petrified at the consequences, but Dad just came up and pulled it out. He never said a word.' Gerald considers that serious matters, either in cricket or domestic situations, brought the best out of his father. 'They didn't faze him. He could take them in his stride. "We'll sort this out" was his approach.'

Johnny was lenient when he realised that his sons' fright had taught them a greater lesson than any he could impose. But unpunctuality incurred withering bouts of anger. The injunction to return home by 8.30pm had to be obeyed to the minute. Gerald, playing tennis with a friend one evening, was delayed by a lost ball, the only one they possessed. The search for it was a prolonged business. He was three-quarters of an hour over the prescribed time limit. Gerald thought he could avoid a reprimand, or worse, a slipper on his backside, as his parents were out at the cinema and would not be home before ten. Gerald's procedure for checking out his safety was to go to the garage door, put his nose in, and smell the heat of the newly-parked car.

> On this occasion I could smell it. Both the front and back doors were locked. I had to face the music and press the bell. The door opened, Dad appeared . . . bump, bump, bump. His foot was behind me as I was hurtled up the stairs to bed.

John Wardle remembers how his father could be mean in small things and generous in others. Gerald says it was really a frugal attitude, a rebellion against waste, which was the result of a stern upbringing. 'Dad would straighten a bent, rusty nail before he would buy a new one. He understood the value of money and he expected his family to show the same appreciation.' Johnny was appalled by what he considered indiscriminate use of lights in the house. The criticism did not slacken even when John and Gerald were married and living in their own homes. As soon as his car turned into their drives there would be a bustle of activity. Fires would be turned down and lights switched off to show that they were economising. His daughter-in-law, Glenys, recalls: 'J. H. would walk into the house and say: "It's like a greenhouse in here. No wonder your plants are wilting with all this heat." ' Johnny had ushered his family out of the pit terraces. The dictum of economy could not be ignored. Every penny had to be stretched as far as possible.

Amid the banter about lighted cigarettes being pulled out of his pockets, there is a lingering gratitude to Johnny for his care and concern in family matters. John Wardle says:

> He did amazingly well by all of us with the money he earned. He did not fritter it away on drinking or other pleasures for himself. Gerald and I were given good bikes when he came back from tours; there were holidays abroad for us on coaching and other trips; and he helped us buy our first cars.

The brusque manner, which repelled other less discerning people, was a facade. Johnny did find small talk irksome; the niceties of the diplomat were not his style. He was always blunt and forthright and, in the neat phrase of one of his sons, he would never make his sentences last longer than necessary.

Yet the sensitivity of this proud man lay hidden beneath a veil of embarrassment. He was so often in conflict with his true nature, believing wrongly that emotion was a sign of weakness. 'He expected praise but he couldn't handle it,' says Gerald Wardle. 'It was like giving him a Christmas present. He found it difficult to say thank-you. But if he didn't receive the accolades or gifts due to him he was deeply hurt.'

'The worst thing you could have said to Johnny about himself was that he was emotional in what might be construed a soft sense,' comments one close friend. Johnny almost seemed to polish his forbidding image. It was a defiant posture which he felt compelled to maintain in a career which mingled high accomplishment and bitter sorrows.

# 3
# The Marathon Man

> *'The weak state of Yorkshire's attack has meant that Wardle has been overbowled. Originality and experiment in his bowling had, of necessity, to be replaced by negative attack.'* – Bill Bowes.

YORKSHIRE'S deep distrust of the eccentricities of wrist-spin, a form of attack which ironically troubled them greatly over the years, was a disquieting experience for Johnny Wardle. That he conformed to an illustrious left-arm tradition in taking 1,846 wickets at less than 19 runs each for Yorkshire and England is a measure of his perseverance at odds with his natural inclination as a bowler.

In terms of strict accountancy and the tried and trusted tenet of orthodoxy, Yorkshire were perhaps right. Wrist-spin was, in their view, not a commercial proposition on the generally soft wickets in the north. Wardle himself, in later years, accepted the restriction. 'The wickets were generally too slow for the unorthodox method of attack,' he said. He estimated that less than 200 of his wickets fell to the wrong 'uns.

Yet the prejudice against wrist-spin is repudiated by many eminent judges, including Jim Swanton and Jim Laker. It was their belief that Yorkshire denied themselves the best of Wardle. Johnny's prowess as the left-handed purveyor of chinamen and googlies was only challenged in English cricket, by George Tribe and Jack Walsh, both Australians. And if you discount the occasionally profitable spells of Denis Compton and Maurice Leyland, he is unique in this accomplishment as an Englishman.

The late Bill Bowes, as the Yorkshire bowling coach of that time, denied allegations that Wardle was discouraged from bowling wrist-spin.

We had been trying to get Johnny into the Yorkshire orthodox tradition. But we soon realised that the best plan was to allow him to mix them. On turners he got the ball to bite with his orthodox slows. On good wickets he was able to achieve movement with his wrist-spin. At that time it was amazing how few batsmen on the county circuit were able to 'tell' him.

Bowes, like Sir Leonard Hutton, believed that the element of surprise in the use of wrist-spin was the key to Wardle's success.

> There were always three or four cheap wickets for Johnny at the end of the innings. He didn't have to change his field because the batsmen did not know which way the ball was going to turn. He could slip in his chinaman or googly without being punished.

Bowes said they retained the normal orthodox field setting for Wardle's unorthodox slows and did not change it unless the wickets were hard and firm in England.

Raymond Illingworth, as one of Wardle's younger Yorkshire colleagues, remembers Johnny's tremendous skills as a wrist-spinner. 'He would go for a month without bowling it. But when he did, he'd win matches for us.'

Sir Leonard Hutton has also paid tribute to Wardle's talents as a master of bowling varieties. He recalls his confusion during a Yorkshire net practice following the 1946–7 tour of Australia.

> Wardle joined two other young bowlers who were bowling to me in the nets. He bowled orthodox left-arm spinners to me for quite some time and then without a word of warning produced a chinaman to be followed a few balls later by the googly, both pitched on a perfect length. The chinaman turned considerably and the googly enough to beat the bat. 'That surprised you,' called Johnny from down the net. Not only was I surprised, I was elated and my thoughts turned to the outstanding talent of this young cricketer. I was so impressed by his natural cricketing ability.

Wardle also remembered how he had foxed his renowned Yorkshire senior. 'I don't want to sound immodest, but I have never made such a great player look so much at sea.'

Hutton's puzzlement should have ensured a greater use of Wardle's diverse talents, which flowered gloriously in his international swan song in South Africa in 1957. Had Wardle's mastery as a dual-purpose bowler been allowed to ripen earlier, it would have stifled his growing resentment and perhaps made him unassailable as England's left-arm spinner.

Yorkshire's seeming tardiness in acknowledging Wardle's versatility is defended by Norman Yardley, his captain from 1948 to 1955. Yardley would have liked to recruit another left-arm bowler as good as Wardle but one who was purely orthodox. Johnny could then have been employed as an attacking rather than as a stock bowler. Wardle was, by force of circumstances, the marathon man in a threadbare county attack before the arrival of Bob Appleyard and Fred Trueman.

The lamentations over the death of Hedley Verity wailed on like a sighing wind in the post-war years. Wardle had to shout to make his voice heard above the requiem for a cricketing artist. Ted Lester, the present Yorkshire scorer and a close friend and colleague of Wardle's at that time, says:

> Johnny was crucified by the Yorkshire press who couldn't accept that he was different from his predecessors. Rhodes and Verity didn't need to bowl chinamen, so why should he? Did he think he was a cut above them? And when things went wrong, as they will with any spinner, and he got some tap, they were twice as hard on him.

One display of ferocious hitting by Peter May was the signal for a critical fusillade in Yorkshire press circles. Johnny recalled:

> Peter sorted me out on a bad wicket at the Oval. I don't think Surrey got more than 180 and he got a hundred of them, 80 or 90 off me. He refused to move away from me. I reckon I would have bowled the others out as fast as they came in if I could have got at them. All he did when I pitched up was to hit as hard as he could. He was dropped three times, twice at slip off thick edges. But they were sharp chances.

Wardle marvelled at the fury of May's onslaught:

> He hit me over extra cover for six; he hit me over mid-off for six; and, mark you, this was on a bad, popping wicket. Peter probably let fly and missed two or three times in an over, but when he hit it he really hit it.

Back home in Yorkshire the pundits were scandalised by the treatment of their left-arm bowler on a spinner's wicket. Wardle was roundly abused for his prodigality and for being outsmarted by the dictatorial Surrey batting master. 'What they didn't realise,' said Johnny, 'was that nearly all my bowling was at May. He was a tremendous player, Peter, and he sorted me out that day.'

Wardle made his debut for Yorkshire in a friendly against

Derbyshire in August 1945. Appropriately it was on his home ground at Bramall Lane. It was the first county match to be played at Sheffield since before the war. Johnny bowled only eight overs in the match, but he enlivened the proceedings with a flurry of boundaries, including three sixes, in both his innings. First, in company with fellow colt, Alex Coxon, he hit 64, defying veteran campaigners, George Pope, Cliff Gladwin and Bill Copson. In the second innings, after a major stand between Hutton and Watson, he built on their lead with another batting assault before being dismissed two runs short of another half-century.

His championship debut came in the following season against Worcestershire at Leeds. Five runs were needed for victory when he joined Frank Smailes at the wicket. He was an unknown number eleven and some Yorkshire members looked at him appealingly before retreating to the back of the pavilion. 'They couldn't stand the tension,' recalled Johnny. 'There were three balls to go off one over from Jackson. I pushed defensively at two of them and then edged the third between wicket-keeper and slip for two runs.' Smailes, at the other end, obtained another fortuitous two, edging Howarth through the slips before making the winning hit. 'It was only as we crossed for a third run that we realised we only needed one, so great was the excitement.'

Wardle had no time to dwell on this thrilling Yorkshire victory. He had to change quickly and rush by taxi to Eccleshill for a Priestley Cup match at the Bradford ground. He arrived there to find that the match had already started and he was next man in. He was just able to buckle on his pads before the wicket fell and out he went. 'I thought it was known in Yorkshire by this time that I liked to hit the ball,' said Johnny. 'But when I took guard the fieldsmen were crouching round the bat.' The fielders withdrew after he had circumspectly defended the first ball. Johnny was puzzled by the relaxed pressure until he was told that he had stopped a hat-trick. On the next evening he took six wickets for 12 runs to guide Eccleshill to victory in the final.

In 1946 Wardle was waiting in the wings for the call to spin as Hedley Verity's successor. He was not alone among the hopeful aspirants. Occupying centre stage in that season was the wily veteran, Arthur Booth who, more than a decade before, had failed in his claim for the privileged position as Yorkshire's slow left-arm bowler. Booth was now 43 and almost as old as senior county players, Wilf Barber and Maurice Leyland, who had returned to the side after war service. In his first full season in first-class cricket Booth headed the national bowling averages with 111 wickets at a cost of 11.61 runs each to help Yorkshire secure yet another championship. It was an impressive farewell by the genial Arthur, who fell prey to a rheumatic illness and had to retire from the game in 1947.

Wardle was not an automatic choice to succeed Booth. 'There is no harder position to fill in the Yorkshire team than that of the slow left-arm bowler,' wrote Yorkshire historian, Jim Kilburn. 'Because of the great ones that have gone before the standard of any successor is expected to be very high indeed.' Wardle was to discover just how formidable was his task. Hedley Verity's elevation to the role was immeasurably helped by his rapport with Wilfred Rhodes and the influence of a great cricketer. By contrast, Wardle was sadly deprived of Verity's guidance during his formative years with the county. 'People will compare me with Hedley and that makes it hard going,' said Johnny. 'I am not a Verity and never shall be.'

Jim Swanton, in his appraisal of the respective merits of Verity and Wardle, says:

> You would want Hedley on your side because you could always be sure of a minimum performance from him. If he had anything to help him, he could be very dangerous. In all circumstances he would be steady. Johnny, on a bad day, could be expensive. But if matters went well for him – if he had wickets that took wrist-spin – he could be a good deal the more dangerous of the two bowlers. He also spun it more as an orthodox slow left-hander than Hedley.

At the beginning of the 1947 season, with Booth unfit and clearly not a long-term candidate, Alan Mason, the Addingham colt, was given first chance to press his claim. Yorkshire decided to give Mason and Wardle six games each before making their choice. 'Mason bowled beautifully in the Yorkshire tradition, not giving anything away, but he did not take many wickets,' remembers Ellis Robinson, the former Yorkshire off-spinner. 'Then it was Johnny's turn and down came the rain.' Wardle grasped his opportunity.

He was awarded his Yorkshire cap in August. It was one of three given on the same afternoon during the match against Gloucestershire at Bradford. Another recipient was Gerry Smithson, a talented left-hand batsman who scored 98 in a Roses match and was selected along with Wardle for the 1947–8 tour of the West Indies. The third cap went to Don Brennan, a superb wicket-keeper who later played for England and offered a serious challenge to Godfrey Evans in a career curtailed by business commitments.

This triple selection by Yorkshire had only occurred once before, in 1934, when Frank Smailes, Cyril Turner and Ken Davidson received the distinction. Wardle, then aged 24, did not secure his place in the team until mid-June. By the end of the summer he had taken 86 wickets at a cost of 25.46 runs apiece and won a place on the MCC tour. *The Cricketer* commented: 'Wardle has improved rapidly and he bids fair to become a worthy successor to Yorkshire's imposing line of slow left-arm bowlers.' Of his bowling in the match against Surrey at the Oval, one correspondent wrote:

> It was a long distance affair of 50 overs. Two easy catches were dropped off him, but he took four wickets for 91. He showed an ability and stamina to keep a length on an unyielding wicket that was reminiscent of J. C. White and Hedley Verity.

Bolstered by this praise, Johnny's composure was only slightly ruffled by a batting extravaganza at the Scarborough Festival. Freddie Brown rattled up a quick-fire century. Wardle's figures were 3 wickets for 236 runs! It reinforced his view that batsmen, not bowlers, should do the bowling at Scarborough. It was much less important to them in the final averages.

Recalling his Yorkshire promotion, Wardle said:

> I had an early success against Somerset which gave my confidence a great boost and earned me an extended run in the team. Two further successes against Surrey and Middlesex obviously put the cat among the pigeons when Arthur Booth declared himself fit. We both played in the team for four games. The reason for this move was to enable the selectors to judge me against him under exactly the same conditions.

The decisive match which confirmed Wardle's status was against Nottinghamshire at Trent Bridge where he passed a searching examination with flying colours. Brian Sellers, the Yorkshire captain, considered that Booth had shepherded Johnny through his stern test. Booth bowled 54 overs for 74 runs and 2 wickets at one end; and Wardle emerged with figures of 2 wickets for 119 in 55 overs. 'I came out of this marathon fairly well,' recalled Johnny, 'and that was the end for Arthur for whom I had the greatest respect. I naturally studied him all the time and was most impressed with his rhythm.'

Bill Edrich, an effervescent bombardier, was the scourge of Yorkshire in Bill Bowes' benefit match against Middlesex at Leeds in June 1947. He hit thrillingly, hard and often, for 70 and 102, the only scores above 50, in a match dominated by bowlers. The second-day wicket was one which lingers in the dreams of slow bowlers. While most of his team-mates faltered disappointingly, Wardle took

7 for 66 in 36 overs, including the wickets of Compton and Robins with successive deliveries.

In the late 1940s Yorkshire were in the throes of a taxing team-rebuilding programme after the retirement of Leyland and Barber after one post-war season and Bowes in the following year. Sellers remained as captain for two seasons, and he was to exert a powerful influence in Yorkshire cricket circles as an administrator over another two decades. The sadness, for many people, was that this great champion of Yorkshire cricket found himself increasingly at odds with a changing world and thought he could still apply the same standards as he did before the war.

Like his post-war counterpart, Stuart Surridge, the Surrey captain of the 1950s, Sellers had flourished because of his absolute command. In the 1930s, in a different economic climate, the virtues of loyalty were so much a part of the fabric of life that to question them would have been unthinkable. The words of Bill Bowes, in his heyday as a Yorkshire professional, were attuned to the intense competition within his own team: '*None of us* would be good enough to captain Yorkshire.' Herbert Sutcliffe, presented with the opportunity of the Yorkshire captaincy as long ago as 1928, had acknowledged the dilemma when he gracefully declined the honour. For all their wealth of experience, Sutcliffe, and probably later his protégé, Leonard Hutton, accepted that in the Yorkshire context they could not distance themselves sufficiently from their fellow professionals to assert an impartial rule.

In his brief post-war reign as captain, Sellers was suddenly presented with a crop of eager but raw recruits. He could be as sharp as the most caustic drill instructor, and perhaps he had to be. The nickname, 'sergeant major', was freely used out of his hearing. Wardle remembered his old captain as a strict but just disciplinarian and told the story of one pre-match lecture by Sellers. 'You've got to concentrate on every single ball of the match,' the Yorkshire captain told an awed assembly, 'and still have enough concentration left to keep an eye on me.'

The tribute paid by Jim Kilburn to Sellers is a telling assessment. It exemplifies the characteristics shared by Sellers and Wardle and reveals the accord that could have existed on the field in a longer relationship. Kilburn wrote:

> No captain was ever more proud of his players. No captain defended their interests more steadfastly once they had proved themselves worthy members of the team. He was ruthless in his demands. His discipline was considered harsh and sometimes he was less than

tactful, but his mistakes were those of a man with the strongest sense of duty. He never courted favour nor feared unpopularity and he never shirked a task.

Johnny Wardle always required strong but sympathetic leadership. Sellers' retirement at the end of the 1947 season deprived him and other Yorkshire youngsters of improving government. 'If Brian had been in charge for another five seasons, Johnny would have been an entirely different kind of person,' says Ted Lester. He contends that the rash of disagreements which later spread through Yorkshire's ranks would not have been countenanced by Sellers.

On one occasion at Headingley, Sellers, with Johnny in tow, marched his young pupil around the ground in the rain. The disciplinary parade, with Sellers flourishing his umbrella and Wardle struggling to keep up with his captain's raking stride, must have been an entertaining sight. Sellers vigorously held forth on the standards expected of a Yorkshire player. At the end of the blistering catechism Johnny was told (expletive deleted) to clear off and behave himself. Wardle had to count to ten on that day and he would have continued to rein in his temper if Sellers had remained at the helm.

Inheriting the mantle of Brian Sellers was an unenviable task. His successor, Norman Yardley, a distinguished cricketer of proven quality and tactical acumen, was perhaps too kindly a man to curb the wilder exuberances of his team. 'There was no comparison between Brian and Norman as cricketers,' says Ted Lester. 'Yet when Norman was away captaining England and Brian stood in we won a lot more matches. Everybody pulled together and we knew what we had to do.'

The seeds of the insecurity which was to bedevil Wardle's career were sown at an early age. Even after he had been awarded his Yorkshire cap his bowling was considered too inaccurate to satisfy the purists. The message was bleak and threatening. Other left-arm challengers, Alan Mason, Johnny Ashman and Ronnie Wood, battled unsuccessfully to oust him during these critical years.

'If Johnny did not almost make himself indispensable, if anyone came up half-likely to take his place, his position was in doubt,' says one sympathetic friend, Charlie Lee. 'He could not afford to have a bad season or even a bad month. If you were not of a philosophical nature Yorkshire could ruin you mentally.' Lee remembers one conversation with Wardle during a cricket journey to Chesterfield. 'Dost tha' know why ah'm playing for Yorkshire?' asked Johnny. Lee thought it a strange question but he replied: 'No, but you're going to tell me, aren't you?' Wardle turned to his companion and said: 'Because ah'm best bloody left-arm bowler in Yorkshire. If I wasn't, they'd have me out tomorrow.' It was the response of an embattled cricketer who was constantly having to prove himself.

The charges laid against Wardle were that he did not bowl sides out in favourable conditions. When he did take wickets it was said that the batsmen had played suicidal shots or surrendered in abject fashion. Bob Appleyard, his later spinning partner, believes that some of the criticism may have stemmed from the fact that Johnny did not always adopt an offensive approach. 'But you must remember that Johnny was being judged by the highest standards, the highest in the land.' Ted Lester contends that Wardle could have quashed the objections had he been allowed to bowl his wrist-spin on those days when orthodox methods did not prevail.

> We had a sufficiently strong batting side for Johnny to bowl his wrist-spin. His wickets might have cost a little more although the wrong 'uns were rarely collared. He would have taken his wickets a lot quicker. And this would have improved our chances of winning matches.

Bill Sutcliffe, son of Herbert and Yorkshire's captain for two years in the mid-1950s, is steadfast in his admiration of a gifted bowler.

> Johnny slotted in perfectly after the war. I looked upon him as a typical Yorkshire professional similar in attitude to those of the great pre-war era. He was a very mean bowler in his early days. The only way you might have faulted him was if you were trying to bowl a side out and he had taken the first five at little cost. Then he might have bowled maidens instead of pressing home his advantage.

Sutcliffe believes that Wardle fully measured up to the Yorkshire bowling method of tidiness and immaculate line and length.

> You cannot afford to concede runs too early. Pressure has to be applied on the opposition. Johnny was an intelligent man. He knew when the time was ripe to introduce his chinamen and googlies as a surprise tactic and without changing his orthodox round-the-wicket line of attack. He would either bowl them at the tailenders, or when we had a big lot of runs on the scoreboard. Then he had more licence to bowl his wrist-spin. He could afford to be more indulgent as a bowler.

Brian Close pays tribute to Wardle as a bowler of genius, a master of variations of flight and pace and a player who always thought soundly and responsibly about his plan of action. Johnny appraised his own merits in the following words:

> Four and five overs, me with the stock ball so that I could bowl one a little slower and get the batsman caught in the covers. That's why he could not be allowed to get a single to relieve the tension. We had to stop that single. . . . When I thought the batsman was sizing me up and getting ready for a charge I would toss the ball a little higher, dropping it a foot shorter at the same speed, and hope to get him caught – a caught and bowled or a catch in the covers.

Wardle remembered how he had seven or eight different paces and how he used to study his opponents all the time. 'It's all done by body action and the position of your hand at the top determines whether the ball comes out quick or slow. You've got to bowl with a quick action to deceive the batsman.' Warming to his strategy theme, Johnny said:

> You can release the ball at the same speed and you can bowl six different deliveries. You let the ball go at the same pace but you release it a little further back. Then you go a bit further through with it and it's still the same pace. But it is bowled at six different trajectories.

Brian Close says that on good wickets Wardle would often drop a fieldsman three-quarters back, behind square-leg for one specific ball. 'In the middle of a spell of orthodox stuff he would suddenly slip in the googly about the line of the leg stump. The batsman would go to sweep, hitting against the spin, and more often than not the ball would go straight up in the air to the fielder.' On one occasion in a Roses match at Old Trafford the Lancashire captain, Nigel Howard, came to the wicket just after Wardle had snared a colleague in this manner. Howard walked across to have a word with the other batsman, Ken Grieves. He told Grieves: 'Watch Wardle with this funny stuff and cut out that legside shot. He's fooled too many people with it.' Howard did not heed his own advice. Off his first ball he holed out to the man at square-leg.

Wardle's baffling enticements as a wrist-spinner produced an amusing interlude in a Gentlemen versus Players match in the Scarborough Festival. Bill Sutcliffe was opposed to his Yorkshire colleague and the victim of Johnny's artfulness. Sutcliffe was armed with Wardle's earlier disclosure that he could not bowl the googly with a low arm action.

I was about 40 not out when Johnny came on to bowl at the Trafalgar Square end. He pitched what I thought was his chinaman – his arm was way down – around the leg-stump. I was just ready to hit it over the pavilion when the ball turned the other way and took my off-stump. It was his googly, of course. It was just so ridiculous. Johnny looked down the wicket at me. He just laughed and laughed.

Away from the festival frivolities Wardle shouldered a heavy burden in the 1940s, carrying an attack which, in the words of one observer, would not have flattered a reputable club side. 'We had a right nonsense attack,' said Wardle. 'I'd go on after two overs, and that was me till the close of play.' In one season he pounded through 1,800 overs and wore out three pairs of boots.

Norman Yardley says Wardle was first change in any conditions. As Yorkshire juggled with an unprepossessing assortment of trundlers, Johnny was even called upon to open with the new ball. 'Get loose and take the shine off before you start spinning,' was the instruction given to him.

Wardle, as will be seen, was never slack or work shy as a bowler. 'The only trouble was getting him off,' says Yardley. In 1948 Johnny bowled 1,247 overs and headed the Yorkshire averages with 148 wickets at 18.46 runs apiece. Against Essex at Westcliff he had match figures of 12 for 160, including 7 for 88 in 37 overs, in the victory by 7 wickets; at Lord's he took 8 for 105 in the innings win over Middlesex; there were 13 wickets in two matches against Surrey as Yorkshire notched a notable double over their southern rivals at the Oval and Sheffield; and 6 for 17 in the rout of Sussex at Bramall Lane. Only three bowlers, Muncer (Glamorgan), Pritchard (Warwickshire) and Walsh (Leicestershire) took more wickets than Wardle in 1948. 'Though there were days when he bowled very well indeed, there were others when his analyses reflected little credit on opposing batsmen,' was the judgement of Jim Kilburn. Yorkshiremen are not given to fulsome praise, even sometimes when it is warranted, but this was hardly an encouraging verdict.

Don Bradman, triumphant again on his last tour of England in 1948, offered a more pleasing assessment of Wardle's potential. 'This was my first encounter with Verity's successor, Wardle,' said Bradman. 'I studied him closely and must say he bowled impressively. There was the usual immaculate length, direction perhaps astray at times, good spin and a deceptiveness of flight more reminiscent of Rhodes than Verity.' It was estimated that Yorkshire dropped at least seven catches as the Australians struggled in their first innings at Sheffield. Wardle's return for the innings was 20 overs for 37 runs and 3 wickets. It included the prize one of Bradman.

Wardle remembered his apprehension at coming face to face with the great Australian.

> I expected an instant hammering from a batsman whom I regarded as the finest of them all. I set an orthodox slow bowler's field of one slip, three on the legside to save singles and the rest in the covers. My first ball was pitched around leg stump and Bradman played it with a fantastic sweep. He appeared to be letting the ball go harmlessly by, then suddenly, at the last possible fraction of a second, he hit it an almighty crack with an almost vertical bat, and it seemed to whistle past the leg-stump and hit the boundary rails simultaneously. My next ball was a better one. I should think it pitched on a good length well on the middle stump, and it was cracked past mid-on for two. It was the long grass at the football end, rather than any fielder, that saved the four. The third ball, which I again thought to be of perfect length and direction, went scudding past mid-on's other hand for three.

There was a hasty conference with Norman Yardley before Johnny next bowled to Bradman. Yardley explained that the shot past mid-on was one of the Australian's most punishing strokes. Wardle recalled:

> Our plan was to transfer a man from the off to the onside. I was still to attack the leg and middle stumps, hopefully inviting a drive to the weaker offside. After two hard on-drives which failed to pierce the close-packed field, Don then decided to hit me through the covers. As it turned out, I had flighted this ball a bit more than the previous ones, and instead of a cover drive, he put up a dolly catch to the skipper.

In his second innings Bradman was less accommodating in a second-wicket partnership of 154 with Bill Brown. 'What's happening, Johnny?' called out Yardley after one especially punishing over. Wardle replied: 'They were all right, skipper, when they left this end.' Bradman, who was not a man to scatter compliments like confetti, did not forget the persevering South Yorkshireman. 'Throughout the tour no other bowler of this type worried us with flight to anything like the same extent as Wardle.' It was a tribute which made Johnny flush with pride.

Yorkshire, against all expectations, shared the championship with Middlesex in 1949. This was the season when Wardle had to take stock of his talents. Alan Mason was given a further chance to take over the position as slow left-arm bowler. Johnny, in the words of one friend, was 'put out to grass' with Bradley Mills in the Huddersfield League. 'Johnny showed his character in that season. He had been virtually told he wasn't good enough.'

Well-meaning attempts had been made by Bill Bowes, the Yorkshire bowling coach, to remodel Wardle's action and correct the chest-on approach at the point of delivery. Wardle was advised that it would be in his own and Yorkshire's interests to revert to the orthodoxy of Rhodes and Verity. The ideal, he was told, was the cartwheel action – the arm coming round like the rim of a wheel for perfect direction – and to do that he had to achieve a sideways-on action as he came in to bowl. Wardle was either unwilling or unable to assimilate the lesson. He lost both form and confidence. 'It took me weeks of practice to get back to my own style and individuality and begin to take wickets again,' he said. As a footnote to this unhappy experience, Trevor Bailey says today that Wardle's action was not attractive although it was very good for his wrist-spin. This comment perhaps helps to explain why Yorkshire wanted to change his action.

Johnny swept back to prominence in 1950 and produced what he believed was his finest bowling performance in his orthodox style, on a good wicket against Middlesex in June. He took 8 wickets for 26 runs. Middlesex were routed for 78 in their second innings and Yorkshire were remarkable victors by 229 runs.

'There were those in the pavilion who were wearing their white roses in something like the old style – the style of the 1930s,' commented a *Yorkshire Evening Post* correspondent. Jack Robertson, as obdurate as ever in a crisis, had hit a century to defy Yorkshire and save the follow-on. Yorkshire then sped to a declaration with 158 in 100 minutes. Wardle hit 40, including six fours and a six. He then measured up his opponents for the execution with the relentless pressure which was to become his trademark. There was just one minor blemish to spoil Johnny's happy June day at Lord's. His figures should have been 8 for 20, or 8 for 21, if you include the statutory single then granted to the beneficiary. Wardle duly lobbed a slow full toss to Jim Sims and was hit for six.

'Wardle bowled beautifully,' said Jim Kilburn, 'and Middlesex allowed him to set a field containing five men within six yards of the bat. Whenever the batsmen guessed they guessed wrongly, and whenever they resolved upon inactivity Wardle pressed them harder and harder until they gave themselves up.'

Wardle really had no need to reproach himself with his opponents' shortcomings. Hedley Verity had not been prone to misgivings either when wickets fell like apples from a tree. Like Hedley, Johnny did not especially rejoice in easy pickings; they simply compensated for those days when wicket-taking was a harder and more satisfactory accomplishment.

Roy Booth, the former Yorkshire wicket-keeper, remembers such an instance when Wardle cast his spell over Nottinghamshire on a plumb wicket at Trent Bridge. By lunch on the last day both sides had completed their first innings. Reg Simpson, undefeated on 50, was serene and confident in the second innings and Notts were cruising to a draw. 'Norman Yardley opened up with Johnny bowling his wrist-spinners after lunch. Johnny proceeded to take seven wickets, including Simpson's, for around 40 runs, and Yorkshire won by eight wickets with 20 minutes to spare.'

The late Bill Bowes, writing in *Wisden*, after Wardle had been named, along with Tony Lock, as one of the Five Cricketers of the Year in 1953, said:

> There is no doubt that the weak state of Yorkshire's attack in recent years has meant that Wardle has been overbowled. With much truth the players named him, 'perpetual motion Wardle.' Originality and experiment in his bowling had, of necessity, to be replaced by negative attack.

One marathon effort, astonishing even by Wardle's own standards of endurance and accuracy, was his stint of 53 consecutive overs for 66 runs and 5 wickets against Middlesex at Lord's in 1951. 'He bowled without rest except for lunch for four hours,' reported the *Yorkshire Post*. 'Wardle kept the chains upon the Middlesex batsmen by good length, variations of pace, and the threat rather than the actuality of spin.' It was a performance of consummate skill and also demonstrated the physical stamina of a supremely fit cricketer. 'Some of the runs to Wardle's expense account were desperately hit. The pitch helped him only in a tendency for the ball to keep low, and he could properly label his success, "all my own work",' added the *Yorkshire Post* report.

Yorkshire owed an enormous debt to Wardle in achieving a runners-up place to Surrey in 1952. Before the season started Johnny must have calculated the strenuous work which lay ahead of him. Fred Trueman was absent for most of the season on National Service and Bob Appleyard was out of action, the victim of a saddening illness. If anyone deserved a championship medal for uncommon zeal it was Wardle.

The extent of his labours are indicated in his final figures which read: overs – 1,847.2; maidens – 810; runs – 3,460; wickets – 177; average: 19.54. Eight times during the season he secured 8 or more wickets in a match, and three times he took 10 or more – 11 for 98 against Kent at Canterbury; 10 for 118 against Kent at Leeds; and 10 for 96 against Somerset at Huddersfield. Wardle's best individual feat was reserved for his supporters at Bramall Lane, Sheffield. He took 7 Middlesex wickets for 49 runs in the course of 213 balls.

Wardle must have considered that he had passed a gruelling examination. Instead he was left to scratch his head in puzzlement at the critical reception. The wavering praise defied explanation in cricketing terms. It seems certain that he had an uneasy relationship with the Yorkshire media. Such phrases as 'he can climb and fall like a barometer in a typhoon' and 'he spins the ball more dangerously than any other bowler of his type now playing yet sometimes his close-in fieldsmen live nervous lives' paid scant regard to his work in difficult circumstances.

The marathon man of 1952 took more wickets than anyone else in the country. Jack Young (163 wickets), Alec Bedser (154) and Cliff Gladwin (152) were his closest rivals. For Yorkshire Wardle and Close bowled nearly 2,500 overs between them and took 256 wickets to exceed the tally of 16 other bowlers tried during the season.

Wardle's monumental efforts took Yorkshire to the brink of another title and only Surrey's remarkable consistency deprived them of the honour. Yorkshire, in fact, gained eight more points (224) than Warwickshire had achieved in winning the championship the previous season. Yet, despite a late surge, they still finished 32 points in arrears. It was the beginning of an era of fierce rivalry, a trial of strength tilted in favour of Surrey because of their depth of talent.

# 4
# Alliance with Appleyard

> *'You either got the buggers out or stopped them scoring. It used to break our hearts if they scored a run off us. It was bloody cut-throat in those days. The runs were hard to come by off Bob and me.' – Johnny Wardle.*

A TERRIFYING machismo gripped the Yorkshire dressing-room like a pestilent plant in the turbulent 1950s. It was no place for soft hearts, with such highly competitive cricketers as Johnny Wardle, Bob Appleyard and Fred Trueman contending for honours. They fought as fiercely with each other as against their often distraught opponents.

A picture of a conflict as savage as a Scarfe cartoon is presented by observers both inside and outside Yorkshire. If this grotesque situation really existed, it has receded in the memory of Bob Appleyard.

> We had our disagreements off the field, but we were a happy side, absolutely united out in the middle. The combative spirit was not as high-powered or as antagonistic as was portrayed in the national press who were looking for sensational copy

Leadership, complacent and frail in discipline, is cited as the prime cause of the supposed disaffection. Norman Yardley, as Yorkshire's captain for much of this period, has been criticised for not extending his authority in a more vigorous manner. Jim Kilburn said of Yardley:

> There is no arrogance of conquest or dictatorship within him. His leadership must inevitably include the limitations of his outlook. He

can rule with co-operation but not by overriding authority, and he expects the response of adult intelligence and behaviour. He is most successful where the ethics are not in dispute, and he omits the expression of blame more often than the quiet word of praise.

Here we have a masterly description of a sportsman which goes to the root of Yardley's captaincy.

Appleyard maintains that it would be a mistake to believe that Yardley's easy and friendly manner indicated a lack of toughness.

> Norman led from the front. He could bat and bowl and get wickets when necessary. He was a courageous fieldsman close to the wicket. Everybody respected him as the complete cricketer. Without him I would not have got anywhere in first-class cricket. Norman must be the best player Yorkshire has had as captain.

There is an equally vehement defence of Yardley as a motivator. 'None of us needed to be motivated. We were Yorkshiremen, that was enough. We had learned our cricket the hard way in the leagues. We came into the side battle-hardened.' Appleyard remembers his former captain as a man who did not wield the big stick. 'He would hold the carrot in front, which suited me. For someone like Trueman, in his immature days, a lash or two from Sellers might have been the best for him.'

The bowling alliance of Wardle and Appleyard was one of the most feared combinations in the land. It first prospered in Appleyard's magnificent opening season in 1951 when he took 200 wickets at a cost of only 14.14 runs each. He finished top of the England averages and bowled Yorkshire to second position in the county championship. He was then aged 27, and comparatively unknown. His achievement was regarded, in Yorkshire circles at least, as the most sensational performance by a debutant since the days of Wilfred Rhodes.

Despite Appleyard's short career, broken for two seasons by debilitating tuberculosis, the late Bill Bowes rated the Bradford-born off-spinner as one of the three outstanding bowlers he had seen in his lifetime. The others were the legendary S. F. Barnes and Bill O'Reilly, the Australian. Bowes recalled Appleyard on trial in the Yorkshire nets. He told Arthur Mitchell, the county coach: 'I can't teach this lad anything. His action and control is good, and he spins the ball.' From his first appearance in the nets, commented Bowes, Appleyard was the complete bowler. With his smooth, high action, using all his 6ft 1½in, he opened the bowling with fast-medium inswingers. As the ball lost its shine, he intermingled slower off-spinners.

Norman Yardley says that Appleyard's chief asset was his direction. 'On the "stickies" he often bowled with just two fieldsmen on the offside at extra cover and mid-off. His line was so good that we didn't need a man behind for the ball slipping outside the off-stump.' Jim Swanton says that Appleyard had a distinctly individual talent, 'I cannot think of a close parallel to him as a bowler. He had a deadly accuracy and the ball was sharply spun and cut.'

Wardle also laid stress on accuracy in his tribute to his bowling partner.

> In his first year he was a medium-pacer, with a very good quicker ball. Bob was dead on line – leg stump or middle and leg – and straight over the top. He also had the ability to vary his pace without the batsman being aware of it until it was too late. He sometimes bowled like Alec Bedser and sometimes like Jim Laker and you scarcely realised the difference until you were out.

Johnny ruefully admitted that he helped Appleyard as much as anybody towards his achievement in 1951. His figures for Yorkshire, in a season of wet wickets, were 99 wickets at a cost of 19.27 runs each. *Wisden* commented: 'Wardle enjoyed his days of triumph but he did not always exploit conditions in his favour.' Appleyard exonerates his partner from blame.

> I was bowling fast off my middle finger and I had to dig the ball in to obtain any response. In this way I was able to slightly penetrate the surface and the ball would lift and turn. Johnny spun it all right but the ball just slipped through off the top.

As a pair of bowlers, Wardle and Appleyard generally fitted each other like two well-worn gloves. The gauntlets, to stretch the metaphor, might occasionally have been thrown in the dressing-room, but once the pair got their boots on and were out on the field any quarrels were forgotten in the pursuit of wickets. 'The great joy of bowling with Johnny was when we were both bowling well and we knew it,' says Appleyard.

The worst feature, as far as Appleyard was concerned, was that Wardle bowled his overs so fast. Johnny bowled off two or three paces. Bob's run-up stretched over 16 yards. Wardle was once timed to bowl an over in 59 seconds and he rarely exceeded two minutes. 'We reckoned to bowl two overs in five minutes,' says Appleyard. 'I had hardly time to get my breath back at the other end.'

Bowling on good wickets was their chief delight. On the turners it would be an insult to their skills if they did not take five or six wickets. The happiest moments of combat were on plumb wickets when everything was in the batsman's favour. It was then their job to pin the good players down and prevent them from gaining a winning position.

The frustration would mount as the batsmen failed to pierce the field and the unyielding pressure eventually produced mistakes. Appleyard says: 'You can't do this on your own. If the chap at the other end is giving fours away, the batsmen don't need to bother about you.' Johnny and Bob tried hard to follow the advice of Emmott Robinson, the Yorkshire sage. Emmott once said: 'Concentrate on five good balls an over and make sure that the sixth isn't a bad 'un.'

Wardle and Appleyard were intensely proud Yorkshiremen. 'We didn't like to lose,' says Appleyard. 'It was unforgiveable for Yorkshiremen. The first time I was on a losing side I thought the world had come to an end.' Johnny reinforced the point in one of our conversations. 'You either got the buggers out or stopped them scoring. It used to break our hearts if they scored a run off us. It was bloody cut-throat in those days. The runs were hard to come by off Bob and me.'

He illustrated the Yorkshire hostility in his peak years with a story of a match against Sussex at Park Avenue, Bradford. This particular piece of belligerence nettled a normally stylish stroke-maker and the most pleasant of men, Les Lenham. 'Bob wasn't playing in that game,' recalled Wardle, 'but Fred was in the team and we had a more or less international attack.' The Sussex batsman survived the barrage for a few overs before he finally perished, perhaps thankfully, and returned to the pavilion. He was met on the stairs by the injured Frank Lowson who had watched his ordeal in the middle. 'Bit of good experience that, weren't it?' suggested Lowson. Les replied: 'Good experience! They're at you all the time out there. They don't give you a thing. They begrudge every run you get.'

Bob Platt, one of the emerging Yorkshire bowlers during the reign of Wardle and Appleyard, remembers the rivalry of his two seniors. 'It was an education to watch them bowl on a turner. The ball always seemed to go to a fieldsman.' Platt recalls one instance of their keen competition in a match at Chesterfield.

> Johnny and Bob were involved in earnest talk between the overs. The ball was turning and they were both on at the *wrong* end. They were arguing about which way the wind was blowing and which end was taking spin. After listening to this exchange for some time, Bill Sutcliffe said: 'To hell with this nonsense.' He put Ray Illingworth on and he took six wickets.

## Alliance with Appleyard

Appleyard was usually given priority as a bowler because of his predictability, according to one Yorkshire elder. Wardle considered it an affront if Illingworth or Close were preferred to him and then came on to take wickets. Platt says the arguments between Wardle and Appleyard, however heated, were dictated by a common purpose to overcome the opposition. 'Johnny's attitude was that Yorkshire had to bowl the buggers out twice. He would want his five or six wickets and he might tell you off for running out No 10.'

In 1950 Appleyard played in two matches for Yorkshire's first eleven against Scotland and Surrey. In the game at the Oval he bowled Fletcher for eight, Peter May for nought, and finished with four wickets for 47 runs. He recalls:

> I realised that I wasn't good enough as a fast-medium bowler. I could bowl an off-spinner. At the Oval, after about five overs, I ran up and bowled a slow spinner. The batsman had a tremendous swipe at it. It pitched and turned and knocked his middle stump out. The dismissal was amazing to me and even more so to my own side. No one had seen me bowl off-spinners.

Norman Yardley was among the astonished observers. 'Make your bloody mind up,' he told Bob. 'How can I set a field when you're bowling like that? Your best bet is to stick to your off-breaks and slip in the odd seamer.' Yardley encouraged Appleyard to practise his spinners at the county nets in the following year. Bob, a determined and thoughtful cricketer, showed his application to the new method when he sustained a blister on his first finger. He changed to bowl his off-spinners from the middle finger. 'I found I could bowl it a lot quicker, almost at full pace, and with greater power and control.'

In July, 1954, after Wardle had taken his 1,000th wicket to become the tenth Yorkshire bowler to achieve this feat, Bill Bowes wrote:

> He has carved a niche between a matchwinner and a first-rate stock bowler that deserves commendation. He will bowl for hours [Johnny also said that he would be disappointed if he did not get his full quota of overs] and has convinced every batsman in the country that he can win any marathon effort intended to tire him out.

Wardle was at his most irresistible in the rout of Sussex at Hull in June. He took 16 wickets in the match for 112 runs, his finest performance in his unorthodox style. His figures were the best by a Yorkshire bowler for 19 years. The previous best was 16 for 35

(8–18 and 8–17) by Bowes against Northamptonshire at Kettering in 1935. 'It was a very slow and easy paced wicket,' said Wardle in recalling his exploits at Hull. 'I decided to try my chinaman the last ball before lunch. John Langridge was playing quietly for the interval, and there was less chance of the ball being dispatched to the boundary. I pitched it a couple of feet outside the off-stump. Langridge padded off and he was bowled round his legs.' One report commented: 'Langridge, after two hours of typical watchfulness, was left inelegantly strokeless.'

Wardle took 9 for 48 in the Sussex first innings and 7 for 64 in the second innings, as Yorkshire won by an innings and 120 runs. He also scored 66 not out, including 10 boundaries in the Yorkshire total of 352. Of Wardle's batting, the *Yorkshire Evening Post* commented: 'He made the runs when they were wanted, and in a fashion which said once again that he could, without a deal of difficulty, build a claim for a batting place that would give him the chance of the double.'

In the first innings Sussex were 67 when the second wicket fell and there was no subsequent stand worth more than 37. Wardle's 26 overs were consecutive and, said one report, 'only Sussex ever wanted him to be taken off'. Johnny thoroughly enjoyed himself against batting which was increasingly marked by hysteria. 'Wardle, of course, had no concern with the epidemic of batting eccentricity, except to induce it and spread it,' reported Jim Kilburn. 'He was well enough suited to be allowed scope for experiments in spin and length, and the more obviously uneasy the batsmen became the more elaborately did he feed their uneasiness.'

On August Bank Holiday Monday at Old Trafford, Wardle was even more remorseless in the overthrow of Lancashire. Play did not start until a quarter past four after the ground had been flooded over the weekend. In two and a half hours Lancashire collapsed from 30 for 2 to 73 all out. Wardle bowled unchanged and bowled again immediately when Lancashire followed on.

Wardle's first innings figures, the best of his career, were: overs – 21.2; maidens – 12; runs – 25; wickets – 9. On the Monday afternoon he took 7 wickets for 17 runs from the 101 balls he bowled. He became the first Yorkshireman to take 9 wickets against Lancashire since Emmott Robinson secured 9 for 36 at Bradford in 1920. Alan Wharton (41) scored over half the Lancashire total and no one else reached double figures on the spiteful Old Trafford wicket. It was a bowling performance of complete domination and one to be relished all his days. It had an especial sweetness in this particular setting.

## Alliance with Appleyard

Lancashire were dismissed for 137 in their second innings, Appleyard this time taking the major share of the wickets with 7 for 33. Wardle's return was 3 wickets for 60 runs. Yorkshire's victory by an innings and 38 runs was the first over the old enemy since before the war.

Wardle won the bowling prize of 100 guineas for his performance against Lancashire. One Red Rose wit said he should share the money with the Old Trafford groundsman, Harry Williams, for getting the wicket fit for play. Having earned the money, Johnny was disinclined to surrender it to a fellow Yorkshireman. Fred Trueman was a late challenger for the award. He had advanced to 8 wickets for around 20 runs in a match following Wardle's triumph at Manchester.

Bill Bowes' account reflected Johnny's dilemma as the prize was slipping from his grasp. 'The last two batsmen were together. Johnny was fielding at square-leg and Fred was bowling. This batter hit a catch, a nice comfortable one, which Johnny would normally have swallowed. He put it down.' Bowes said it might have been an uncharacteristic error, except that it did unfortunately coincide with Trueman's bid for the money. Someone remarked: 'Nay, Johnny, whatever were you doing?' Johnny replied: 'If I'd caught it, Fred would have taken the brass.'

For a time in the 1950s Trueman and Wardle, vexing as they were for their captains as colleagues, were nevertheless Yorkshire's main attacking force in the absence through illness of Appleyard. Trueman was always likely to turn the course of a match with a devastating spell of fast bowling. Wardle was the indefatigable drill, boring into the rock of so many opposing innings.

The competition between the two South Yorkshiremen was often a source of hilarity as they each strove to outdo the other as batsmen. Both were ferocious hitters against bowlers short of genuine pace. Even Frank Tyson, at his fastest, was unable to force a truce between them. In one match at Northampton Trueman had become progressively more angry as Tyson cut a swathe through Yorkshire's batting. Tyson was then the man in charge as England's fast bowler. Fred was a little out of temper. He thought it would help his cause if he cut his rival down to size.

Wardle was the first to face the music, an overture as tempestuous as any orchestrated by Stravinsky. He backed away from his stumps as Tyson hurled the ball down at him. He flailed his bat with the flourish of the village blacksmith. The stumps scattered in all directions. Fred, next man in, met Johnny as he returned to the pavilion. 'What sort of a bloody shot do you call that?' asked

Trueman. Wardle did not reply as he hurried past him. Fred was determined that he would not suffer the same fate as his colleague. Tyson raced in again. Fred stood resolutely in defence, all three in front as he thought, but over went his off-stump. Johnny was waiting for him when he walked forlornly into the Yorkshire dressing-room. He could barely conceal his pleasure. 'What about that then, Fred?' he said. Trueman bristled with anger as he replied: 'I slipped in the mire you left behind you.'

Yorkshire are sometimes charged with taking their cricket pleasures too seriously, and in the 1950s the belief still persisted that the county had an inalienable right to the championship pennant. The triumphant march of Surrey, seven times champions under Stuart Surridge and Peter May, only served to heighten the criticism of the team. Bill Sutcliffe, the former Yorkshire captain, says he was immune to such criticism. His father, proud in his memories as a distinguished Yorkshire and England batsman, could not accept the failures. 'Herbert,' says Sutcliffe in a reference to his parent, 'thought it was a disgrace for Yorkshire to finish second or third. I gave up too young. He made me sit down and write a letter of resignation.' Bill was an amateur and his promotion to the Yorkshire captaincy in 1956 was an accolade which had delighted the elder Sutcliffe.

The severity of the outcry and exaggerated claims that the Oval wicket was tailored for the spin of Jim Laker and Tony Lock reflected the incredulity and distress in Yorkshire. Bill Bowes believed that Yorkshire lacked the bowling strength to match Surrey, who had bowlers for all conditions, both at the Oval and on other grounds. Sir Leonard Hutton endorsed the verdict of many people that the Surrey team was powerful enough to bear comparison with the great Yorkshire side of the 1930s. Bob Appleyard expresses the view that if Yorkshire had played all their home matches at Park Avenue, Bradford – a notoriously helpful wicket – they might have been in the same situation as Surrey were at the Oval.

The narrow divide in talent between Yorkshire and Surrey can perhaps best be judged from the fact that the two counties between them supplied 13 players to England in one season. The essential difference was that Surrey had a pool of loyal and experienced reserves in their second team which enabled them to maintain their supremacy. Yet Yorkshire were four times runners-up and third on two occasions during the 1950s. Appleyard's absence for two seasons and injuries to other key bowlers diminished their championship challenge. Other contributory factors were inconsistent batting and an inability to find another bowler to help Trueman in his opening thrusts.

Johnny Wardle's finest season, statistically, was in 1955 when he took 195 wickets at a cost of 16.14 runs each. 'Wardle, making more use of the left-hander's off-break than previously, bowled extremely well,' commented *Wisden*. Tony Lock, his left-arm rival, exceeded this tally with 216 wickets for an average of 14.39. In the Surrey ranks Stuart Surridge had only to mention Wardle's name (and another tumble of wickets in Yorkshire) to produce a renewed surge of aggressive bowling from Lock.

The closeness of this contest was paralleled in the battles for the championship between Yorkshire and Surrey. Hutton, having stepped down from the England captaincy and on the brink of retirement, played in only ten championship games in 1955. Appleyard, after beginning the season in fine style, suffered a shoulder injury and played in only three matches after June. Despite these handicaps, Yorkshire made Surrey fight hard for their fourth successive title. This feat had only twice previously been accomplished under the same captain. Yorkshire, led by Brian Sellers, were the champions in three seasons immediately before and one season after the war. Alfred Shaw captained Nottinghamshire in their run of four titles from 1883 to 1886.

In 1955 – a summer of glorious weather – Surrey set up a new record for the number of championship points since the system of awarding 12 points for a win and four points for a lead on the first innings was introduced in 1938. They recorded 23 victories out of 28 games to total 284 points. Yorkshire won 21 games and totalled 268 to beat their previous highest score of 260 achieved in 1939. They finished just 16 points behind Surrey.

The struggle for mastery between the two counties dominated the season and Surrey did not shake off their rivals until the end of August. They traded success with success throughout May, each winning their first six games. Against Gloucestershire at Bristol Wardle took 6 wickets for 6 runs in two balls less than 10 overs, as Yorkshire won by an innings. There was some astonishing cricket on a rain-affected pitch at Bradford. Yorkshire beat Northamptonshire by 78 runs in only seven and a half hours of actual playing time. George Tribe, the Australian left-arm bowler, secured 15 wickets for 75 runs, including 9 for 45 in Yorkshire's second innings, and still finished on the losing side. It took the combined efforts of Wardle (7 for 38) and Appleyard (11 for 48) to counter Tribe's teasing wrist-spin. Tribe was to exact blissful revenge at Northampton three years later with figures of 15 wickets for 31 runs, including 8 for 9 in the second innings, and this time Yorkshire had no answer.

At the beginning of June fortune turned against Yorkshire in Arthur McIntyre's benefit match at the Oval. On a treacherous wicket Surrey won by 41 runs, but not without being given a fright. Yorkshire finally succumbed within twenty minutes of the safety of a draw. Appleyard, making his off-breaks rise wrist-high, took 7 wickets in Surrey's first innings. His challenge was met by the double thrust of Lock and Loader with 4 wickets each.

Yorkshire's lead of 47 runs on the first innings became a deficit of 216 as Fletcher and May built up a match-winning partnership. Sutcliffe, Wilson and Watson stoutly defended Yorkshire's cause. They ensured that there would be no rout by following the classic principles of bad wicket play. They either pushed forward to stun the spin, or hit hard when hitting was possible. 'With victory growing closer, Surrey themselves delayed it,' reported the *Yorkshire Post*. 'They began to drop catches and in dropping catches began to bowl with more vigour than control.'

Wardle revelled in this disarray. He pulled Lock for six and skied the next ball steeple-high to mid-wicket, where he was missed by Laker. He next struck Lock for another six and escaped a stumping before Bedser bowled him. Trueman and Appleyard lasted nearly half an hour before Laker at last accepted a catch off Lock to Surrey's relief.

A fortnight later there was a gleam in the eyes of the Yorkshire members in the Headingley pavilion. It was 'summat like', in the White Rose vernacular, to see cock-a-hoop Surrey mastered by six wickets. A thrilling struggle between the two leading sides in the country drew over 60,000 people, and the atmosphere resembled that of a Test match. It was Surrey's first loss in 16 consecutive games, denting a record which stretched back to July in the previous season.

The gates were closed on the Saturday when Surrey staged a spectacular recovery after losing 8 wickets for 119 runs. Yorkshire looked the champions, Surrey the uncertain challengers until mid-afternoon. By a combination of misfortune and misjudgement Yorkshire surrendered their advantage. It was pulled away from them by tail-end batsmen. Lock, at number nine, scored 55; Loader, at number ten, scored 81; the ninth wicket added 96 runs, the tenth 53. 'Some of them were lucky runs from the edge of the bat and some were from skied mis-hits to untenanted parts of the field,' reported the *Yorkshire Post*. 'Once or twice the ball missed the stumps by those margins that lead bowlers to premature old age.'

At one point in the partnership Trueman, goaded beyond endurance, hurled a fierce bumper at Lock. It was a ball which would

## Alliance with Appleyard

have decapitated the Surrey man had it struck him. Lock glared at Trueman and lifted his bat in a threatening gesture. He stalked three parts of the way down the wicket and tapped an imaginary spot. It was an amusing touch but Wardle slyly capped it. He sauntered up, took off his cap and, with immense dignity, bowed his head over the mark.

After their early alarms, Lock and Loader became increasingly confident and selective in their shots. Wardle had taken the earlier wickets of Fletcher, May and Laker. He was, surprisingly, not called upon to bowl as the partnership gained momentum. Instead, he was left to patrol the outfield when his slow spin would have presented more problems than short half-volleys from tired fast bowlers.

Yorkshire trailed by 102 runs on the first innings, but hope still burned after a furious bowling assault by Trueman and Cowan in near-darkness on the Monday evening. There were no light meters to ration the dismay of the Surrey batsmen. Peter May said the light was the darkest he could remember playing in England. 'The umpires stoutly refused to go off – to the delight of a large and noisily jubilant crowd. The light on the scoreboard was described in the Surrey dressing-room as shining like a beacon on the Eddystone lighthouse.'

In an hour and 40 minutes Surrey lost 7 wickets for 27 runs. Trueman's figures were 3 for 18 and Cowan's 4 for 4. Lock, battered from foot to shoulder, was the courageous and unbeaten 'nightwatchman'. The heroics were in keeping with the compliment paid to him by one Yorkshire player. 'Lockie would be the man you would want alongside you in the trenches.'

Before a third day crowd of 17,500 – the biggest at Headingley for many years – Yorkshire completed a handsome victory. The target was 178 in three and a quarter hours. The winning hit was made by Willie Watson with only ten minutes to spare. The tensions of the day, as Surrey sought to check the run rate, communicated an anguish which perhaps can only occur in a North-country cricket assembly. One misguided gentleman stood up in the stand just as Lock was about to bowl to Watson in the dramatic last hour. He was told to 'sit down' in a manner which suggested that he would be instantly lynched if he did not obey. He dropped like a log on the steps, his sandwich bags strewn beside him, and stayed there in distinct confusion until the match was over.

Johnny Wardle and Tony Lock had much in common as entertainers and competitors in their cricket attitudes. The rivalry which existed between them epitomised the cut and thrust of the Yorkshire-Surrey matches of the 1950s. They both projected a box-office charisma which masked their quiet, serious temperaments.

They were characters in the happiest sense of the word. Johnny's appeal rested in his engaging buffoonery, while Tony, unfailingly ebullient as a bowler and brilliant short-leg fieldsman, held attention with the bravura of a melodramatic thespian.

It was, as Jim Laker has said, a marvellous prospect to see Wardle or Lock bowling to each other. Tony was the bowler when Johnny came out to bat in his benefit match against Surrey at Bradford in 1957. The field spread out for the single traditionally 'given' to the beneficiary on these occasions. Lock bowled the usual long hop. Wardle hit it away and jokingly pretended to set off for a second run. As he did so, Lock dived at full-stretch for the ball. Laker said he was sure that he would cheerfully have run Wardle out, given half a chance. The roars of protest which would have sprung from Yorkshire throats on this benefit day would not have worried him one jot.

A bitterness still prevails in the Wardle family at what they consider the injustice of the England selectors. They find it incomprehensible that Lock was preferred as slow left-arm bowler, despite his action which was widely regarded as illegal. It is an intriguing talking point as to which of the two bowlers would have come out on top in an equal contest. But there is no gainsaying the fact that Lock fully exploited his advantage, however unfair, for England's profit.

Wardle strongly resented cheating in any form and the bias towards Lock increased his aggravation. He could not dismiss the iniquity of his exclusion. 'If Johnny had an Achilles heel, it was Tony Lock. He shouldn't have shown it,' comments one Yorkshire contemporary. 'Come on, lads,' Wardle would call out in a beseeching voice. 'Just watch that bastard throwing it out there.'

# 5
# Locked in a Masquerade

*'A ball shall be deemed to have been thrown if, in the opinion of either umpire, the process of straightening the arm, whether it be partial or complete, takes place during that part of the delivery swing which directly precedes the ball leaving the hand. This definition shall not debar the bowler from the use of the wrist in the delivery swing.'* – MCC Laws of Cricket.

A REVULSION against unfair tactics, as practised by Tony Lock, cast a blight on the career of Johnny Wardle. It was an obsession which cut deep into his personality because he fervently believed that standards were being lowered. He was a casualty of a blinkered approach by cricket administrators. His talents as a bowler were devalued in an unequal contest.

Throughout the 1950s a *laissez-faire* attitude persisted towards bowlers with suspect actions. The cries of outrage did not begin until serious injury – a maiming strike or worse – threatened with the arrival of throwers of unbridled speed. Tony Lock, acclaimed as a master of vicious spin, rose to eminence during this regime of lenient stewardship. The umpires of his time, lacking the whole-hearted backing of the MCC, were reluctant to take extreme action and thus imperil a player's livelihood.

Trevor Bailey and Peter May recall a diminished sensitivity in an unfair situation. Those brave umpires who did call offending bowlers were looked upon as publicity-seekers, says May. 'Lock obviously alarmed certain umpires with his quicker ball, which was doubtful at times. But the tendency at the time was to sweep such unpleasantness under the carpet.'

Wardle, as Lock's rival for the position of England's slow left-arm bowler, looked on grimly, counting his missed caps as the favoured

Surrey man enjoyed his illegal advantage. After his retirement from the first-class game, Wardle wrote: 'Lock used to impart tremendous spin with his jerk and never had to resort to flight to get anyone out.' Remembering his own disillusionment as a Test cricketer, he said:

> Some people are sympathetic and say that bowlers will be put out of the game. I contend that they should not be in cricket keeping legitimate bowlers out of the game. Others remark that the slow bowler does not do any harm so why worry about him. My answer is that he gets wickets to which he is not entitled because of his peculiar method of delivering the ball.

The problem of throwing was a cobwebbed skeleton in cricket's cupboard in the 1950s. But it was not a new phenomenon: in the 1890s an injunction was issued to first-class umpires to be very strict in their judgement of bowlers' actions. Among the bowlers under scrutiny were the Lancashire and England fast bowler, Arthur Mold; Tyler, the Somerset slow bowler; Geeson, fast medium, from Leicestershire; and Bobby Peel, one of Wardle's predecessors in the Yorkshire left-arm spinning tradition.

C. B. Fry was another of the 'doubtful' bowlers named by the authorities. Writing in *The Cricketer* in 1954, Fry said:

> The plain difficulty is that in the modern sense nobody has succeeded in framing a satisfactory definition of a throw which umpires are required to no-ball. In point of fact the whole question turns on what is done with the elbow in the action of projecting the ball. But this has not percolated into the drafting of Law 26. This says: 'For a delivery to be fair, the ball must be bowled not thrown. If either umpire is not entirely satisfied with the absolute fairness of the delivery in this respect he shall call and signal no-ball instantly upon delivery.'

Fry argued that nowhere in the laws was there any definition of a jerk or throw. It depended entirely on an individual umpire's notion of what the term signified.

> Suppose the bowler's umpire detects a doubt in his mind but the square-leg umpire does not. We then have two judges appointed as equal in their powers, directly contradicting one another. What it comes down to is, that each umpire is instructed to be judge but if they differ one of them is suddenly whisked away from the bench and treated as non-operative. How's that?

In 1888, when *Wisden* hailed the proposed formation of the first Cricket Council at Lord's, Charles F. Pardon wrote:

> I have watched for many years with interest, and generally with cordial sympathy, the efforts of Lord Harris to improve conditions under which the great game is played. His crusade against throwing was fully justified, and there is today very much less unfair bowling than was the case a few years ago.

Pardon expressed the view that the game should be played fairly and honourably and that cricketers should be above suspicion.

> Prominent umpires have over and over again told me that in their opinion men upon whose style of bowling adverse criticisms have been written, were unfair, but they were not sufficiently sure of support to take the initiative in no-balling them . . .

In 1952 the same position applied, chiefly because, as Norman Preston, the then Editor of *Wisden* maintained: 'No one wants to shoulder the responsibility.' During the summer Cuan McCarthy, the South African fast bowler, was no-balled for throwing while playing for Cambridge University against Worcestershire. Lock was called by the square-leg umpire, Fred Price, the former Middlesex and England wicket-keeper, in the match between Surrey and the Indians at the Oval. Price no-balled Lock in one over and twice in another. An angry Oval crowd kept yelling 'No-ball' at the umpire, who stopped play and lay on the grass until the noise subsided. It needed a firm appeal by the Surrey secretary, Brian Castor, over the loud-speaker to quell the barrackers.

Peter May, who had just come down from Cambridge, was Lock's captain against the Indians. He asked Price for an explanation of his decision. 'We were all amazed. Fred was in no doubt that Tony had thrown his faster ball.' It was the first time that Lock's action had been officially regarded as questionable. 'Why', said Tony, 'should one umpire no-ball me when all the other umpires have allowed me to go on bowling as I please?' He considered that Price should have had the courtesy to give him a prior warning.

The no-ball calls were not, however, entirely unexpected. In the case of Lock's quicker ball – the fast yorker – half the umpires said, in private conversation, that he threw it, but they were afraid to do anything about it. In the winter of 1952 a writer in *The Cricketer* also commented on the throwing incidents at the Oval.

> Unhappily there is one disquieting feature about this young bowler. In his endeavour to impart more spin and to bowl a faster ball he has raised doubts about the legitimacy of his action . . . opinions will vary about the fairness or otherwise of a bowler's action. It is to be hoped

that Lock will be able to eliminate any element of doubt about his delivery without in any way spoiling his skill as a slow left-arm bowler.

After Lock had been no-balled again on the tour of the West Indies, Alex Bannister commented that both the Surrey committee and the player himself should have heeded the warning lights.

> On this important issue they should not have been content to allow matters to slide. It was not something which could be conveniently ignored, but a matter to be tackled straightforwardly in the triple interests of England, Surrey and Tony Lock. To be no-balled on a 'foreign field' was a severe shock for Lock and his team.

Tony Lock became a Surrey professional in 1946. He was recommended to the county by Mr G. S. Bungay, the club's youth team selector. 'I have put Lock in because he bowls so well for a boy of 16, although I am rather dubious of slow left-arm bowlers at the Oval.' This was a pointed reference to the somnolent wickets of the 1930s, irreverently described by Neville Cardus as being 'rolled and doped to stupefaction'. Lock was not destined to suffer the frustrations of the pre-war toilers. He and his majestic off-spinning partner, Jim Laker, revelled in the boon of a transformed Oval. Bert Lock, the Surrey groundsman and no relation, had reshaped the Oval from a prisoner-of-war camp back into a cricket arena. In the process the Kennington ground never returned to its pre-war condition.

In many people's eyes, especially those with a Yorkshire myopia, the new-look Oval contributed greatly to Surrey's reign as champions in the 1950s. 'If Tony Lock had arrived at the Oval in 1930, with all his great dowry of gifts, we should have heard little of him,' said Cardus. 'He owed much to his namesake, Bert Lock. In fact, Surrey may fairly be said to have won the championship seven years consecutively because of Stuart Surridge's leadership, Jim Laker, and the joint Lock coincidence of circumstances.' The presence of Laker, as Lock's county partner, also undoubtedly swayed the England selectors into omitting Johnny Wardle from their teams on many occasions.

Tony Lock gave little evidence of his later supremacy in his apprenticeship years with Surrey. 'He was just a nice little lobber,' says Godfrey Evans. Tom Graveney remembered this unexciting first phase with some amusement. 'It was in the late 1940s and I played against this soft, gentle little floater. It was a case of "down the wicket and help yourself". I never thought he would amount to very much.'

For two years Lock watched and marvelled at Laker's mounting armoury of skills. He was guided in his attempts to achieve greater spin by the guidance of Laker in the Oval nets. In 1951 he was appointed winter coach at a Croydon indoor school by Mr D. A. Lawrence, a local company director. Over two winters at the school Lock spent six days a week giving lessons and improving his own technique. At the school the beam supporting the roof was low-slung and it caused Lock to drop his high action when he tossed up the ball. As he said:

> Though I was not conscious of it at the time, my arm dropped a little in the delivery of the ball. The beam curbed the trajectory of the flight and I started to bowl a little quicker. I also found that by 'digging' the ball into the wicket, I was able to secure more spin.

By 1952 Lock was quite literally a new bowler. The high action had disappeared during the school practices. The unfortunate legacy was a sinister kink in his bowling arm. As John Arlott commented:

> He was now the ultimate destroyer as a spin bowler. He could wrest turn from the deadest of wickets: on anything approaching a spinner's pitch his break was staggering. His quicker balls came at a wicked pace.

One Yorkshire player of the time remembers Wardle's aggravation in a match against Surrey.

> Johnny had been bowling his orthodox slows without any success for some time. Then Lockie came on and turned it square. How did he do this? Well, he was being a naughty boy. It shouldn't have been allowed.

Jim Laker remembered Lock's faster ball, which some people conservatively estimated accounted for 25 per cent of his wickets. 'It would burst through a batsman's defence before he could pick up his bat from the blockhole.' Ted Lester recalls the amazement of his Yorkshire colleague, Vic Wilson, in one confrontation with Lock at the Oval. 'It was like Tyson at his fastest. Vic hadn't got a very high back lift. He hadn't got his bat up before the middle stump was ripped out of the ground.'

Doug Insole, playing for the Rest of England against Surrey, the champion county, at the Oval, was once the victim of this devastating delivery. The Rest were chasing runs against the clock and, after a shaky start, Insole was beginning to score quickly. In Bill Bowes' version of the incident Lock wheeled in and 'with his fast throw knocked all three down. Doug just stood there in disbelief and said to the umpire: "How am I out then? Was I thrown out?" ' Insole, it must be said, does not subscribe to the view that Lock was unduly favoured by the England selectors if the criterion was the choice between two orthodox left-arm bowlers.

Keith Andrew once kept to Lock in a festival match at Torquay. 'It was quite an experience,' he says. 'Lockie needed two or three wickets to reach his 200 for the season. It really was just like keeping to a fast bowler. Lockie was firing them in at a very brisk pace.'

Even in the Surrey dressing-room there were severe doubts about the legitimacy of Lock's faster ball. As Jim Laker puts it:

> Apart from leg-pulling about how well he would throw the javelin, we did not discourage Tony in his new enthusiastic approach to the game. We did not want to undermine his confidence. So many bowlers over the years had got away with throwing or jerking the ball that we decided we were not going to act as jury. It was up to the umpires to decide.

Colin Cowdrey, among Lock's opponents, was a strong critic of Lock's action which, he said, was not limited to his faster ball.

> He looked almost as if he was running someone out from cover point. In the delivery stride he would be seen to drag his back foot, giving the arm time to slow down, curl and bend before banging the ball into the wicket. This had the effect of making the ball leap and cut off certain types of wickets in the most alarming fashion. No other bowler achieved anything like the same result, and one became very suspicious of his action.

It must have seemed to Johnny Wardle that there was a conspiracy to impede his advance as an England bowler. Before the arrival of Lock on the scene Bob Berry, the Lancashire left-hander, had usurped the role. Berry was, it now seems unaccountably, preferred to Wardle for the tour of Australia in 1950–1.

Wardle was bitterly disappointed at his omission from Freddie Brown's side. He had topped the Yorkshire averages with 174 wickets at a cost of 16.7 runs each and scored over 700 runs; he was fifth in the national averages; and only Roy Tattersall, another Lancastrian, with 193, took more wickets in 1950. Johnny was sorely tempted to leave the first-class game and accept a lucrative

## Locked in a Masquerade

offer from a league club. The counsel of Yorkshire friends persuaded him to change his mind, and a Wakefield company came to his aid. They provided him with a winter sales job to help ease his bruised pride.

Sir George ('Gubby') Allen was a dissenting voice among the England selectors who chose Berry for the 1950–1 tour. He considers the selection of the Lancashire bowler was an appalling decision. Allen was also one of the selectors who picked Tony Lock after a secret mission to watch the Surrey bowler in action in Kent. Joining Allen on this outing was fellow selector, Les Ames.

> Les and I walked round the ground and looked at him from every possible angle. What we both said was: 'He looks peculiar but we don't think he throws the ball.' That was our absolute, sincere belief. I would not have picked Lock if I had thought he threw.

Lock must also have satisfied Norman Yardley, the chairman of the Test selectors in 1952, and Leonard Hutton, the England captain, who batted against him in the week before he made his England debut against India at Manchester.

Jim Swanton puts forward a strong admission of regret. 'I think we all in retrospect feel a little guilty about Lock's action. It was common knowledge that he threw quite a few. Although many observers did take this view, there is something different about a slow bowler doing it.' Swanton acknowledges that from a batsman's point of view a slow bowler's illegal delivery is almost as difficult as if it were thrown by a fast bowler. 'The reason, according to those who have played against chuckers, is that you pick up the flight later. This was certainly true of Tony because his faster ball was absolutely lethal.'

George Headley, the great West Indian batsman, then aged 44, was one of Lock's victims in his last Test, the first of the 1953–4 series, at Kingston, Jamaica. 'In the second innings Headley was chucked out by Lockie's fast yorker,' recalls Swanton.

On this MCC tour Lock was also no-balled for throwing against Barbados at Bridgetown. His guilt was confirmed by the action of two umpires. He was twice called in three balls by the square-leg umpire, Harold Walcott, the uncle of the Test player, Clyde Walcott. Later in the same day he was also no-balled by umpire Jordan, standing at square-leg. Of the Barbados incidents Alex Bannister wrote:

> With his faster ball Lock shattered the stumps of the young left-hander, Sobers. The call did not seem to have been made until Sobers

had attempted his hurried but unsuccessful defensive jab. Sobers walked away not realising he was entitled to stay. Neither he nor Dick Spooner, the MCC wicket-keeper, heard the umpire's call. Lock was plainly put out by the incident and he went over to register his complaint to the captain. Hutton heard him, then walked across to umpire Walcott. Hutton knew better than anyone that he could do nothing about the decision. But his action gave time for Lock to simmer down and regain his composure. Hutton rightly protested to Walcott that the call came too late – most people agreed that it was made a split second after the ball hit the wicket – and Walcott, whose efficiency was seldom questioned, replied 'I'm sorry.'

Sir Leonard Hutton, in his recollections of the tour, said the no-balling of Lock had a big effect on him in the West Indies.

Being no-balled for throwing three times in one day unsettled him so much that never again in the West Indies did he try to bowl his fast ball. Consequently the batsmen were not compelled to be always on guard against it. This clearly minimised their difficulties against Lock and decreased his effectiveness.

Sir Leonard thought that Lock was no worse a culprit than West Indian off-break bowler, Sonny Ramadhin, or Australia's Ian Johnson, both of whom jerked the ball even if they did not actually throw it.

If I were an umpire, I would be very careful about taking action unless I was convinced beyond a shadow of a doubt. What may look like a throw from one position can appear to be a perfectly legitimate delivery from another.

Jim Laker welcomed the moves against Lock because he felt that his Surrey partner was far too good a bowler to resort to a ball that was suspicious. As a result of his experiences on the tour of the West Indies, Lock restricted his use of the quicker ball.

England players, including Godfrey Evans, who took part in Laker's historic 19 wickets' match against Australia at Old Trafford in 1956, believe that the record would have eluded Laker had Johnny Wardle been at the other end instead of Lock. Lock's match figures at Manchester were 1 for 106, including 0 for 69 in 55 overs in the second innings. 'Tony was so annoyed with himself that he bowled faster and faster and shorter and shorter,' recalls Evans. 'Johnny, had he been playing, would have taken five or six wickets to upset Jim's applecart.'

Colin Cowdrey remembered a superb piece of attacking bowling by Laker.

> Here at least was one instance where the bowler with the genuine action could boast the greater success. More often than not the reverse is the case. In fact, the most telling argument in being tough on bowlers with suspect actions is that so often the legitimate bowler, who has spent years perfecting his art, is at a disadvantage.

Both Jim Swanton and Ted Dexter have described the events leading to Lock's decision to change his action on the 1958–9 tour of Australia and New Zealand. This was Lock's first visit to Australia. He had increasingly been regarded as inferior to Wardle on overseas wickets; and his late selection for the tour came after his rival had been dismissed by Yorkshire and subsequently barred by the MCC.

Swanton recalls that Harry Cave, the New Zealand bowler, had filmed the highlights of his country's tour of England in the previous summer. The film included the exploits of Lock, who had enjoyed a sweeping success against New Zealand, taking 34 wickets in the series at a cost of 7.47 runs each. Lock attended a screening of the film when the MCC party travelled on to New Zealand in 1959. 'Lock was horrified when he saw himself on film. He came back home determined to correct his action,' says Swanton. Dexter also remembered Lock's embarrassment in the New Zealand cinema.

> We could see the bend in his arm at the point of delivery and several of us gasped out loud. When the lights went up, there was Locky white-faced and silent. The next day, he came to the nets and bowled very slowly, with no sign of the quicker ball.

The revelation on film preceded an intensive period of reappraisal by Lock. At the age of thirty, he was faced with a challenge, amounting to a command, to scrap the action which had made him a Test bowler. He had to replace it with a different delivery which would suppress criticism and satisfy an extra vigilant jury. Arthur McIntyre, his Surrey team-mate, remembered the work Lock put in at the Oval nets.

> He tried all sorts of styles until he hit on the right one. I don't think I've seen a greater trier than Lockie. Sometimes blood would be pouring from his fingers as he slogged away to get it right.

The process of rehabilitation took many months but it led to unreserved praise. Dexter, Lock's captain on the 1961–2 tour of

India, says: 'Lockie bowled superbly for me on that tour. There was all the flight and variations you could wish for.'

The rekindling of Lock's talents and the adjustment to a slower style brought him a late harvest of wickets. He emigrated to Australia in 1963 and led Western Australia to a Sheffield Shield triumph. He also had much to do with the development of future Australian Test players, including Dennis Lillee. Lock spent three years with Leicestershire from 1965 to 1967. At Grace Road his bowling and enthusiastic leadership laid the foundations for an imposing era of success. Within two years he took Leicestershire to second place in the county championship, the best position in the county's history.

Tony Lock's indomitable spirit and ebullience as a cricketer disarmed even those who labelled him a chucker, a bowler with a 'very powerful throw', to quote Godfrey Evans. Lock could also claim his advantage as a brilliant short-leg fieldsman, one of the finest in the history of the game. One incredible effort, against South Africa at Leeds in 1955, remains vivid in the memory. With superb anticipation, he chased a mistimed pull to square-leg and plunged, like a swooping shark, into a headlong dive to take an astounding catch. Neville Cardus recalled Lock holding 'quite sinful catches, catches which were not there until his rapid, hungry eyesight created them.'

Peter May, one of Johnny Wardle's most fervent admirers, and his captain at home and overseas, believes that it was the Yorkshireman's misfortune to play in the same era as Lock.

> Had it not been for Tony, Johnny would have played in practically every match. He was a very high-class bowler and he had the great gift of being able to bowl his chinamen and googlies without seeming to practise them. It was a quite extraordinary accomplishment. I cannot remember Johnny bowling his wrong 'uns to me in county cricket.

May also makes the interesting point that there was a possible case for including Wardle, in his unorthodox style, and Lock, as the orthodox arm of the tandem, in the same England team. 'They were two different bowlers in the 1950s. I believe that you should pick the best bowlers for England regardless of whether they are fast, slow or medium.'

Lock and Wardle themselves also believed that they could have operated successfully as a pair. Wardle, in one conversation, told me:

> Lock and I were anything but similar and there was something to be said for playing us both in the same side. Tony was a very aggressive

type of bowler and he tried to get a wicket with every ball he bowled. I was more patient, using changes of pace and flight to tie the batsmen down. I was prepared to bowl several overs before bowling the delivery I hoped would get me a wicket. There was an even bigger contrast on hard, fast wickets when I bowled in my unorthodox style.

Jim Swanton reinforced the point in one report of a provincial game on the 1956–7 tour of South Africa.

Lock was a hateful proposition with his acute spin away from the bat, while Wardle at the other end was baiting his traps at an entirely different speed and trajectory. Apart from bowling with the same hand, these two have little else in common. In fact, contrast makes them an excellent pair working together.

Bob Platt expresses a Yorkshire view on this insufficiently exploited combination. 'It would have been incredible to watch Lockie's aggression at one end and Wardle's guile at the other. They wouldn't just have been bowling against the opposition; they'd have been bowling against each other.'

More support for the theory comes from Keith Andrew, who recalls that one of Northamptonshire's best teams included three left-arm bowlers – George Tribe (unorthodox) and Jack Manning and Micky Allen (orthodox). 'It is a myth that you shouldn't play two great bowlers of the calibre of Wardle and Lock in the same team. If we can choose two off-spinners, as we have done in more recent times, then why not select two left-handers, if they are different in style?'

At the root of the issue was Yorkshire's reluctance to use Wardle as an attacking wrist-spinner. Trevor Bailey also believes that the answer to the riddle lay in the contrast in styles of the England slow bowlers of the 1950s. 'The contrast between Lock and Laker was considerably more than when Wardle and Laker were in partnership.' On the question of compatibility, Bailey considers that Wardle and Appleyard formed an equally admirable alliance. 'Johnny and Tony were different but England was better served by the balance of the right/left hand combination, especially when good off-spinners were available.'

In his assessment of the merits of Lock and Wardle, Bailey says that the Surrey bowler was at his best in his final phase when he started to 'think batsmen out'. He does, however, insist that during the period of their rivalry Lock held the winning hand as a fast left-arm bowler on wet wickets. 'On a pitch giving assistance, particularly in England when the wickets were uncovered, Lock was far more of a menace.'

On the harder wickets overseas, says Bailey, Wardle was a far more likely prospect because of his more thoughtful approach to bowling. 'Tony would still think he could bowl them out by pitching leg-stump and hitting the off. And that didn't happen.' Bailey reckons that overseas when batsmen realised Lock was just a medium-pacer his opponents did not find him a difficult proposition. The only exception to this was when the wicket was bad and the ball travelled through 'very straight and very quickly'. 'I would have preferred to play against Lock rather than Wardle on perfect wickets overseas. In England it would probably have been a different matter.'

Godfrey Evans, like Bob Appleyard, believes that Wardle became the complete bowler when he switched more frequently to his unorthodox style in the later stages of his career. 'Johnny was in a different category by that time,' says Appleyard. 'He enjoyed bowling his chinamen and googlies more than his orthodox slows. And he was better in this style once he had mastered the form of attack.' Evans remembers how Wardle delighted in foxing his opponents with his wrong 'uns. 'Johnny loved getting the batsmen in a tangle.' He believes that the reason why Wardle was not picked by England more regularly was because the selectors did not choose him to bowl wrist-spinners.

Keith Andrew is also convinced that Wardle would have taken precedence over Lock if he had been used more in his unorthodox style. Andrew recalls that Wardle, like George Tribe, had immensely powerful hands. 'Johnny and George both employed a vigorous body action in bowling their wrist-spin.' Jutting, determined chins were thrust down the wicket in intimidating fashion. 'You almost bowl with your chin like George,' Andrew once told Wardle. He adds:

> Johnny was a great bowler to have on your side. I know that Yorkshire did not want him fiddling about and he did enjoy tremendous success as an orthodox slow left-arm bowler. But he was a brilliant and accurate wrist-spinner; his googly was very difficult to spot; and, in my opinion, he did not bowl it enough.

Norman Yardley and Bill Sutcliffe both subscribe to the view that Wardle was superior to Lock on all wickets. But they do not think the choice of Lock on certain wickets was wrong if his action had passed inspection. Yardley says: 'Lock would not have been half the bowler he was but for his dubious delivery. He was a slow roller rather than a waspish spinner after he had remodelled his action.'

Batting in the garden at his home at Brampton

Johnny (second left, back row) as a member of the Eccleshill team which won the Priestley Cup in 1946

The England player
with his father and
mother, Jack and Jane
Wardle

Sweethearts all their
lives: Edna and Johnny

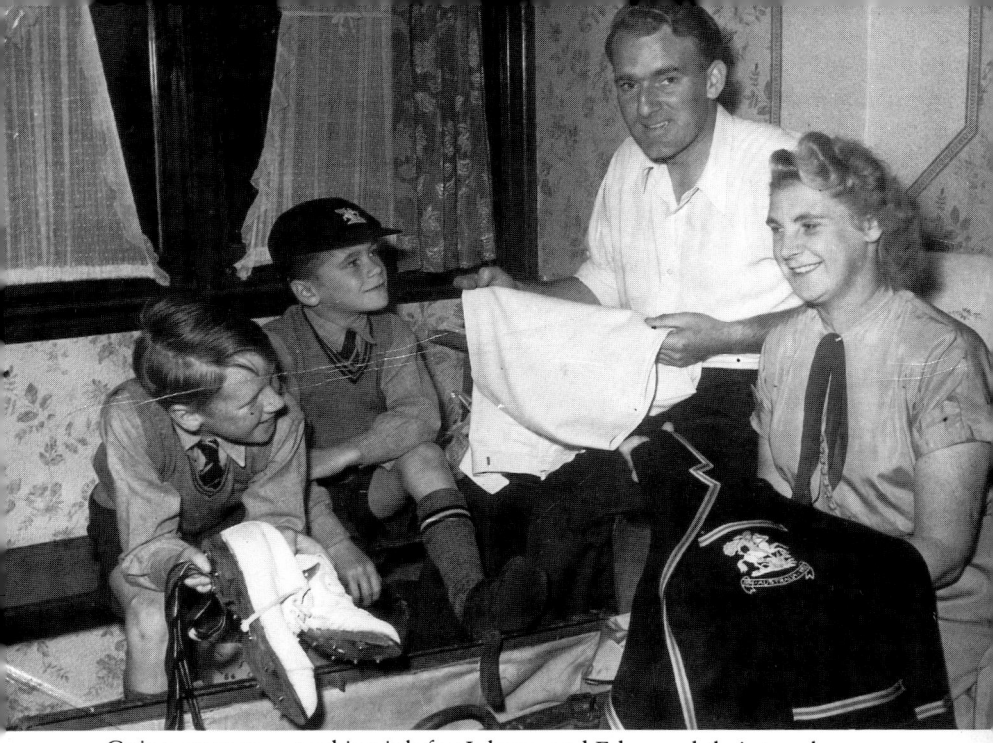

Going on tour: a packing job for Johnny and Edna and their two boys, John and Gerald

Wardle with Brian Close (left) and Freddie Trueman

Yorkshire talents of the 1950s. Back row (l to r): Trueman, Booth, Lowson, Wilson (J. V.), Appleyard, Illingworth, Close. Front row: Lester, Watson, Yardley (capt), Hutton, Wardle

Six-hitter against Surrey: Wardle in ferocious batting action

England captains on parade: Wardle follows Len Hutton (left) and his future skipper Peter May into Test action

Bob Appleyard, Wardle's Yorkshire and England spinning partner. (*Yorkshire Post*)

MCC party which toured Australia and New Zealand in 1954–5. Back row (l to r): Duckworth (baggage master), Andrew, Loader, Graveney, Tyson, Dalton (masseur). Middle row: Wardle, Simpson, Wilson, Appleyard, McConnon, Statham, Cowdrey, Howard (manager). Front row: Bailey, Edrich, May (vice-capt), Hutton (capt), Compton, Bedser, Evans

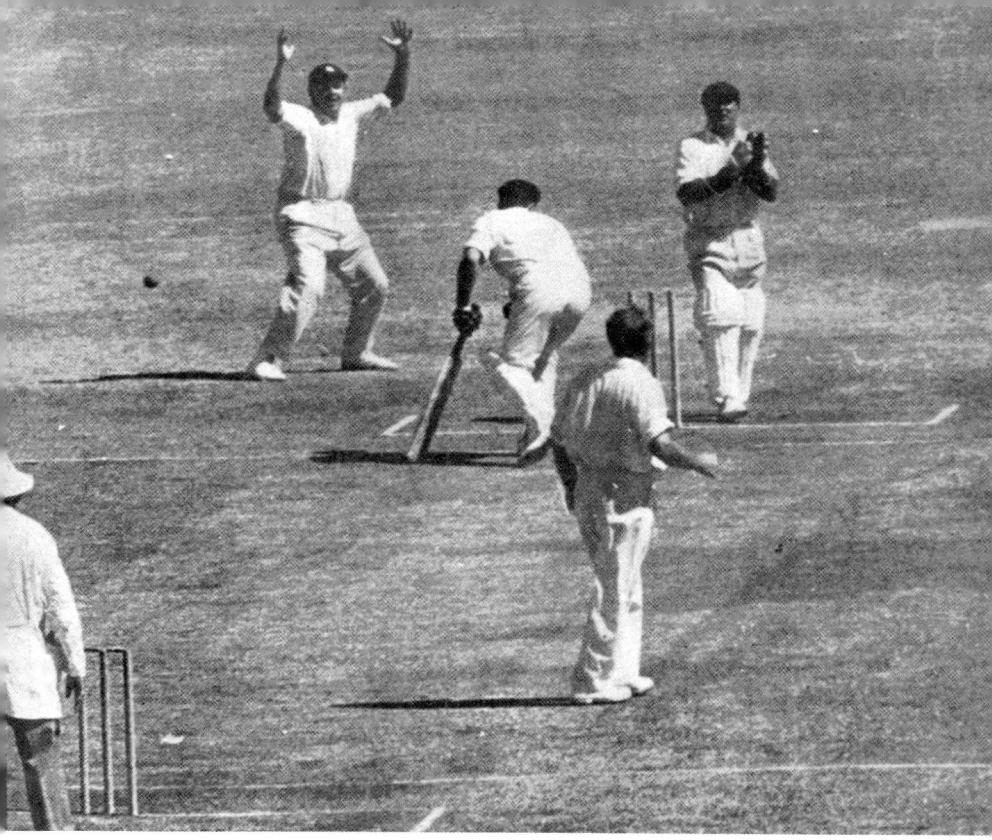

Bowled over by a chinaman: Roy McLean, defeated by Wardle, was one of a succession of South African batsmen baffled by the Yorkshireman's wrist-spin in the 1956–7 series

McGlew in a tangle: the South African captain is bowled by Wardle in the second Test at Cape Town (The South African Library)

Rishton's Worsley Cup-winning team in 1964. Back row (l to r): E. Kennedy, E. Whalley, S. Ormerod, M. Eddleston, K. Flatley, J. J. Smith, D. Lomas. Front row: E. Nuttall, B. Hurst (capt), J. Marsden (president), J. H. Wardle (professional), J. Chew, T. Welsh (chairman)

Norman Yardley, former Yorkshire and England captain

Johnny, the golfer, in action during his retirement

A hole in one: Edna was the star turn in this golfing enterprise

Digging for victory: Johnny, the groundsman at Doncaster

Yardley does, however, consider that Wardle had a tendency to bowl a little short on the 'stickies'. 'When he tried to spin the ball he was inclined to pull it down so that when he really gave it a tweak it was a little short.' Yardley cites the example of the Yorkshire field placing for their great Lancashire rival, Cyril Washbrook, on wet wickets. 'Cyril was a marvellous cutter and we always had a man back at square third-man, to guard against Johnny's occasionally wayward length.'

The criticism represents only the mildest of rebukes for an esteemed bowler; but it does indicate that precision was the cornerstone of the Yorkshire strategy.

> Johnny always thought he could pitch on the leg stump and knock the off-stump out of the ground and, as a result, they used to squirt him down the leg-side. We had to have a man behind square to save runs.

The quality of mercy was strained in Tony Lock's favour in the 1950s. Wardle's bounty, like that of Shakespeare's oppressed Shylock, was diminished by judges who erred, however pardonably, on the side of forgiveness.

The last words on a fascinating analysis must go to a wise man of Yorkshire cricket, the late Bill Bowes.

> Lock threw everything although you would probably pass all of them from certain parts of the field. Wardle was a better bowler – a far more useful man to have in your side – because he was able to come on and bowl his wrist-spin or his orthodox. But you cannot blame the England selectors for going for Lock when he hadn't been done for throwing. You had to watch him down the mid-on line to see the offending action.

Johnny Wardle, the cricket commentator, might have paused to reflect on the irony of the situation during the 1958–9 series in Australia. The Australian chuckers, Ian Meckiff and Gordon Rorke, unpredictable in line and pace, threw out England in a horrendous masquerade. It was a violent rebuff to Tony Lock, their arch destroyer on so many occasions. But this was a cricket counter, brutish and forbidding, which had to be outlawed. These throwers could hurt. The culprits were barred from cricket and their tyrannies quickly dissolved.

The expulsions came too late to reward Johnny Wardle on his pedestal of propriety.

# 6
# Havoc at Manchester

> *'England, thanks to their spin pair, Wardle and Laker, snatched the honours of the match. The collapse showed how vulnerable are our batsmen to a keen attack on a wicket taking spin after rain.'* – Percy Millard, Australian writer

JOHNNY WARDLE, the valiant standard-bearer, ought to have been crowned as England's number one slow left-arm bowler in the Coronation Year of 1953. His mastery against Australia at Manchester, lacking the imprint of an England victory, was judged a hollow conquest. Wardle's discontent seethed like a rebellious tide when he had to surrender his place to Tony Lock in the Ashes-winning team at the Oval.

Wardle was poised to stamp his authority on the Test scene after the eclipse of the Australians at Old Trafford. In the third Test he took 4 wickets for 7 runs in 5 overs to humiliate the tourists in a crazy last hour. The conditions were almost identical to those prevailing in his rout of Lancashire in the following summer. Johnny was convinced that, despite the inevitability of a drawn game, Australia would not have scored 50 whatever tactics they had adopted.

Australia finished the game in an undignified scramble and lost 8 wickets for 35 runs. Until the last phase they had held the advantage but their frailty against spin was mercilessly exploited and their morale undermined to tip the scales, psychologically, towards England.

John Arlott, in his book, *Test Match Diary*, wrote:

> The wicket was, indeed, a difficult one: not an absolute 'sticky dog', but a fairly fast turning pitch ... It is not safe to assume that the Australian innings would have gone down as it did if the position had

been vital. Miller, de Courcy and Lindwall all went making strokes which could not be described as 'business'. Several of the players, too, had scrambled out of their town clothes to bat – with a delay which the crowd bore with little patience. On the other hand, no batsman likes to be shot out in this manner and I am sure these wickets were not deliberately thrown away . . .

Leonard Hutton, England's captain, also rejected the apologia of some of the Australians. He was told: 'Don't take any notice of our second innings. We knew we couldn't lose, so we didn't try.' Hutton replied: 'It wouldn't have made any difference either way; 35 runs was as many as you would have made in any case.'

Australia led by 42 with an hour left to play. The tumble of wickets was irrelevant in the context of the game, but it was an astonishing collapse. Morris was caught in the slips off Laker without scoring; Hassett in the gully off Bedser for eight. Miller was briefly spectacular before being stumped by several yards off Laker for six. Hole, caught by Evans, gave Bedser his 100th wicket of the season. The scoreboard at this stage read: 18–4–2. As John Arlott related:

> It was hard now to believe all this was pointless, the mere playing out of time. As the roar of the crowd rose in pitch and intensity it was an effort of will to relax in the face of cricket apparently so urgent, actually meaningless.

Wardle's introduction into the attack hastened the decline. The fifth wicket fell when de Courcy charged down the wicket, essayed a massive swing at Wardle, and was stumped by Evans. Harvey was bowled for nought and Australia were 31 for 6. Archer was lbw next ball but one. Lindwall swung across the line to hit one four and was comprehensively bowled after another cross-bat heave. Davidson, dropped off Wardle before he had scored, played out a maiden from Laker and the match was over.

Of the second innings debacle, Australian writer, Percy Millard said:

> England, thanks to their spin pair, Wardle and Laker, plus the great Bedser, snatched the honours of the match in the final overs. The collapse showed how vulnerable are our batsmen to a keen, well-directed attack on a wicket taking spin after rain.

Wardle's remarkable analysis was to remain just a cheerful memory as England, without him, regained the Ashes after an interval of twenty years. The allegiance to Tony Lock, who replaced

Wardle at Leeds and the Oval, could not be refuted on figures, even if a considerable number of his wickets were gift-wrapped at the Oval. The weight of evidence also supported the retention of Lock and Laker as a match-winning pair. As a partnership, in five home series in the 1950s, the two Surrey bowlers took 130 wickets between them.

Yet, amid the rejoicing of 1953, Wardle had ample cause to be aggrieved at his exclusion. Lock played in only ten games, eight county games and two Tests, because of an injury to his spinning finger. The injury was so bad at one stage that he only had to bowl four or five overs and the wound would re-open. His position for the conclusive Oval Test was in doubt until less than an hour before the start. He had to undergo hospital treatment on the first morning before being judged fit to play.

Lock and Laker, with 9 wickets between them, were the agents of victory on a highly emotional occasion at the Oval. Lock took 5 wickets in Australia's second innings to make amends for the disorder at Leeds. Australia had been set a target of 177 in just over two hours at Headingley and came perilously close to winning the game. Hutton's attacking gamble, based on the threat of spin, was nullified by over-eagerness on the part of the Surrey bowler. Lock bowled both short and wide and was hit for 48 in eight overs, 14 coming off one over. The Australian charge was checked just in time by Bailey's accuracy and an ultra-defensive spell of leg-theory bowling.

The decision to restore Lock to the England side at Leeds signified an unjust bias towards the Surrey bowler, even if one concedes his greater power of spin and the bonus of his catching. Wardle had batted bravely in the first Test at Trent Bridge where his 29 was the second highest score in England's first innings. At Lord's he had taken 4 wickets for 77, including 3 wickets for 6 runs in 10 balls.

Wardle retrieved a deteriorating situation for England by dismissing Hole, Benaud and Miller. 'He spun and flighted the ball astutely in as destructive and clever a piece of bowling as I have seen in England this summer,' commented one Australian observer. Wardle's figures in this spell were 9 overs, 4 maidens, 23 runs and 3 wickets.

Johnny remembered that his role at Lord's was to restrict runs at one end while England attacked at the other with Bedser, Statham and Bailey. This did not prevent him from twice confounding a respected adversary, Keith Miller. The first innings dismissal was one which always brought a smile to Johnny's face at its remembrance.

I had orders to keep it as tight as possible. I was doing a reasonable job but I suddenly sensed that Keith was straining at the leash. I decided to give one a little extra air knowing that he would have a go. I thought he might mis-hit it for a catch. The ball went into the air all right but the catch was dropped – by a chap sitting on the second balcony of the Father Time stand.

Hutton looked sternly and reprovingly at his fellow Yorkshireman.

The black look I got from the skipper was all I needed to tell me to cut out the rubbish. However, on my approach to the wicket for the next delivery, I felt I ought to try the tactic again. This time I made sure that I didn't overpitch. Keith accepted the challenge again, but this time the ball dipped towards the end of its flight. He hit over it and was bowled.

Wardle's feat at Manchester, a performance of supremely penetrative bowling, ought to have ensured his retention, especially in view of Lock's suspect fitness. The strongly orchestrated argument was that Wardle was limited as an orthodox attacking bowler. His chief merits, said one observer, were his endurance and economy. Judged in this context, there were few better choices in the world, generously pronounced another writer.

One member of the anti-Wardle faction emphasised that the Yorkshire bowler achieved his successes against late order batsmen. The *Yorkshire Post* promptly came to his defence in a wryly amusing leader.

More than 30 years ago one of the most popular cricketing headlines used to be 'Rhodes' Rabbits', the implication being that Wilfred Rhodes' success was largely gained against players low down in the batting order. Johnny Wardle will no doubt be satisfied to be in the company of his even more illustrious predecessor in the England and Yorkshire teams.

Johnny Wardle's Test career began in humiliating circumstances. Wardle, after one season in county cricket, and Jim Laker were among the young players who suffered an unnerving baptism in the West Indies under Gubby Allen's leadership in the early months of 1948. Johnny, in later years, would hold forth in self-mocking fashion on a severely instructive first overseas tour. He took 6 wickets at a cost of 73.50 runs each and played in one Test, the second at Port of Spain.

For the first time in cricket history the MCC went through a tour without a single victory to their credit. Of the eleven matches played, all seven with the then colonies were drawn. The first two of the four Tests were drawn before the West Indies repeated their success of 1935 by winning the last two and the rubber.

Gubby Allen, at forty-five, was the oldest England captain since W. G. Grace in 1899. His role, as one observer assessed it, was a 'trainer of troops'. The 'troops' comprised a collection of unfledged cricketers and a sprinkling of experience in the hands of Godfrey Evans, Joe Hardstaff, John Ikin and Jack Robertson. Jim Swanton comments: 'Poor Gubby had to take this lot with him and found the three "W's" at the other end.' Billy Griffith, the former MCC secretary and Sussex captain, later described the party as virtually England's third team. 'The under-estimated West Indies, with the emerging Worrell, Weekes and Walcott in their ranks, made us pay for our arrogance. Quite simply they thrashed us.'

It was Gubby Allen's view that Pelham Warner was hoodwinked into sending a weak side to the West Indies in the belief that they would not be over-taxed by the opposition. The result was that too many unproven youngsters were selected for the tour. The choice was also influenced by the fact that the better players had undergone a gruelling tour of Australia and New Zealand in the previous winter. The absentees included Hutton (later to join the tour at the urgent request of Allen whose anxieties were not lessened by a spate of injuries and illness), Compton, Edrich, Washbrook, Bedser and Wright. 'We took on more than we ought to have done for the good of the game overseas,' says Swanton.

Dick Howorth, the Worcestershire left-arm bowler, carried an immense burden in the West Indies. He bowled magnificently through out the tour, sending down over 500 overs on plumb wickets upon which he was lucky to see one ball in a hundred turn even a centimetre. Johnny Wardle, as the 'learner' bowler, prudently studied Howorth's technique on the hard, true wickets of the Caribbean and returned home a wiser, if chastened young cricketer.

Wardle, after his initial disappointment in the West Indies, vied with other left-arm candidates, including Lancashire's Malcolm Hilton and Bob Berry, for an England spinning place in the early 1950s. Doug Wright, Roley Jenkins and Eric Hollies were among the last of the outstanding leg-spinners to command Test attention in the post-war period. In the 1950 series against the West Indies, England's spinners were Hollies and Jenkins at Nottingham, and Hilton and Wright at the Oval.

Wardle, in his first Test in England, was selected along with Berry for the momentous match at Lord's in which the West Indies first announced themselves as a cricketing force. Wardle took his first

Test wicket with his first ball. He trapped the West Indian opener, Jeffrey Stollmeyer leg-before-wicket with what was described as a 'length-finder'. He returned to the attack just before the close of play to dismiss Goddard, bowled off his pads.

In 1951 Wardle played in the first of his nine Tests against South Africa at Nottingham and Lord's. He secured five wickets in the two matches. At Lord's, after a thunderstorm in the early hours of Friday morning, Roy Tattersall, the Lancashire off-spinner, brilliantly exploited the conditions to earn match figures of 12 wickets for 101 runs. 'One of the surprises of the match,' reported *Wisden*, 'was the failure of Wardle on a surface more or less made for him. The Yorkshire left-arm bowler was disinclined to pitch the ball up to the batsmen who were able to play back and deal with him.'

The unexpected failure perhaps serves to explain the content of the early criticism levelled against Wardle. It did not, however, take account of the fact that Johnny's attacking edge was blunted by the heavy bowling burden he had to shoulder with Yorkshire in this period. John Arlott laid emphasis on this responsibility in his preface to the 1954–5 tour of Australia.

> Wardle's danger is that he has had too much bowling to do for Yorkshire in the past three seasons, with the result that he has become a more defensive bowler than he needs to be. He has the priceless asset, in a 'natural' left-arm spinner, of being able to bowl the chinaman, and its googly, to a length – a tactic he could, at need, exploit for long spells on wickets which do not help his normal break-away.

It was this versatility which commended Wardle to the England selectors when they chose him, along with Tony Lock, for the 1953–4 tour of the West Indies. Lock played in the first two Tests at Kingston, Jamaica where he became one of the few bowlers to be no-balled in a Test match, and at Bridgetown, Barbados. Lock was undoubtedly disturbed by the censure at Kingston. Jim Swanton observed:

> There is nothing of the patient philosophy about him that one associates with the great left-arm bowlers – the Rhodes, the Veritys and the Blythes. He seems perpetually angry, either with himself, with the batsmen, or the world in general. A proper hostility in a bowler is a good thing but Lock's outraged feelings react against his skill. It is hard to think that he was the same person who had bowled out Australia at the Oval six months before, or who indeed had previously bowled so well on this tour.

The West Indies were the victors in the first two Tests to complete a sequence of five successive wins, in two series, over England. Wardle's inclusion in the MCC team against British Guiana in Georgetown in February, 1954 signalled the turn of the tide. Watson and Graveney both hit double centuries in the MCC total of 607. Wardle, in only his second first-class match of the tour and bolstered by the weight of runs, took 6 wickets for 77 runs in 39 overs. The MCC won by an innings and 98 runs.

'The manner in which Wardle bowled over the wicket, attacked the off-stump, and repeatedly changed his flight, pace and spin should have been a lesson to Lock at the other end, who continued to bowl as he does in England,' commented one correspondent. Jim Swanton also thought Wardle's bowling was a positive gain in the Georgetown match:

> Ever since the tour began, the English attack has been gravely in need of someone who really gave the ball air, and in doing so posed problems similar to those Ramadhin and Valentine set the English batsmen. While Lock toiled in vain, Wardle bowled over the wicket, mixing his orthodox slow left-arm deliveries with off-breaks bowled with wrist-turn and also googlies, which in the case of a left-arm bowler are leg-breaks.

Johnny Wardle's often under-rated talents as a batsman, which later gained him renewed praise in Australia, helped provide the stimulus for England's victory by nine wickets at politically troubled Georgetown. This was a resolute victory achieved amid the fury of the crowd incensed at a run-out decision given against the local hero, Clifford McWatt. The trouble began as the eighth wicket pair of McWatt and Holt took the West Indies score nearer the 286 needed to avoid the follow-on. As Alex Bannister reported:

> By the time the stand had reached 98 the crowd were clapping and cheering madly. Then McWatt struck a ball towards the legside boundary and, either under-rating the fielding abilities of Peter May or caught up in the frenzy of the crowd, he turned for a second run which would have brought up the 100 partnership. It was never on. When McWatt began to try and race back to his original end May had the ball in his hand. Peter threw him out by at least two yards. McWatt acknowledged the umpire's signal by running on towards the pavilion.

Within two minutes of the incident the ground near where the square-leg umpire Menzies was standing was littered with bottles.

For 10 minutes not a ball was bowled. Players and umpires stood there surveying the growing mess. Then Denis Compton tossed a bottle back to the edge of the boundary and Johnny Wardle raised a laugh by picking up another bottle, pretending to take a drink and feigning intoxication.

The chairman of both the Georgetown Cricket Club and the British Guiana Board of Control, Stanley Jones, came on to the field as mounted police ringed off the section of trouble-makers. After a conversation with the chairman, Leonard Hutton waved his team back to their fielding positions. He indicated that, bottles or no bottles, play would be resumed. His reported response to the anxious official was typically courageous. 'No, we'll stay,' said Hutton. 'We want another wicket this evening because we mean to win this match. These people are not going to put us off.'

Hutton's tenacity as a captain was matched by his vigilance as a batsman in England's first innings at Georgetown. His timely score of 169, which charted the course of victory, was his first hundred of the tour and his eighteenth Test century. He found an able partner in the promoted Wardle, batting ahead of Bailey. The strategy was quick runs in a match which England had to win to save the series. The Yorkshire pair added 79 in an hour and a half before a tired Hutton made his first mistake and was caught by Worrell off Ramadhin. Wardle's share was an immensely valuable 38. Johnny sealed his happy recall by England in taking 3 wickets for 24 runs, his invincible chinaman bowling Atkinson, leaving Graveney and Watson ample time to take a leisurely route to victory.

Tony Lock was preferred to Wardle in the drawn fourth Test in Trinidad. The Yorkshireman was called up again to join Lock and Laker in the spinning trio in the decisive final Test at Kingston, Jamaica. Trevor Bailey, in one of the finest bowling performances of his career, took seven wickets to set the stage for victory at Kingston. Hutton, supported by Wardle and Evans in two century stands, built hugely on Bailey's success. The England captain was again the batting bulwark with a magnificent double century. Wardle's dashing 66, his highest score in Test cricket, spilled over with a zest which seemed to relax his Yorkshire colleague.

Wardle hit Ramadhin for two mighty fours in the first over sent down to him. Hutton matched him in adventure by straight-driving a ball from Atkinson for six far out of the ground, and then two balls later struck again with a glorious stroke high over extra cover to the boundary. Wardle responded by lifting a ball from Ramadhin out of the ground and almost as far as his captain's shot off Atkinson.

In two hours between lunch and tea England scored 146 and advanced their lead to 251. Hutton reached a classic double century with a superb cover drive off Sobers. He batted for 8 hours and 24 minutes; his runs came out of a total of 369; and he hit one six and 22 fours. The Yorkshire pair added 105 runs before the stand ended when Hutton at last fell to a catch by McWatt off Walcott. Trueman and Laker shared seven wickets as the West Indies were bowled out for 346, leaving England another modest target of 71 runs.

Johnny Wardle revelled in the infectious joy of his Caribbean hosts. There was a two-day public holiday when the MCC team visited the Leeward Islands. In a carefree atmosphere Wardle won the hearts of the crowds with his clowning, bowling and big-hitting. His adoring fans christened him 'The Duke of Antigua'. For the first time on this tour, against West Indian batsmen often bemused by his wrist-spin, he grew in confidence as he realised the handsome profits which could be garnered from his extravagances.

In Jamaica Johnny pulled off a celebrated catch which Tony Lock would have been proud to claim as his own. Jim Swanton recalled this agile feat. 'McWatt off-drove Laker full off the middle of the blade, apparently between extra-cover and mid-off. Wardle moved to his left as the ball was hit, made six yards at a range of 40, and picked up the ball ankle-high.'

Wardle ousted Lock as England's slow left-arm bowler in the four-match series against Pakistan in 1954. He played in 12 successive Tests, including four in the 1954–5 series in Australia, before surprisingly losing his place to Lock in the third Test against South Africa at Manchester in July 1955.

Wardle headed the England bowling averages with 20 wickets at 8.80 runs each in the series against international debutants, Pakistan, in 1954. In his first and only Test at the Oval he took 7 wickets for 56 runs. His triumph was devalued by complacent England batting. Pakistan's medium-pace bowler, Fazal Mahmood, took 12 wickets for 99 runs in the visitors' victory by 24 runs. Fazal's feat at the Oval gave him a personal niche in cricket's hall of fame. It also fuelled an enthusiasm which was to set Pakistan on a path to greater glory in the years ahead.

Before the Oval reverse, in a bleak summer of rain-affected wickets, England's spinners had threatened to overwhelm the inexperienced tourists. In the first drawn Test at Lord's play was limited to eight hours. Heavy rain washed out cricket on three successive days. In Pakistan's first innings of 87 Wardle took 4 wickets for 33 runs in 30 overs. He conceded only 21 runs in 21 overs.

## Havoc at Manchester

Bob Appleyard, returning to first-class cricket after two years' illness, was paired with Wardle in the second Test at Nottingham. They shared 11 wickets in England's innings victory. Appleyard made a dramatic beginning in Test cricket with seven wickets and assured himself of a place on the MCC tour of Australia in the following winter. 'A bowler taking four wickets for six runs in his first five Test overs must have a place in cricket's story, but there should be many more pages awaiting the adornment of Appleyard's name,' commented Jim Kilburn.

In a spell of 26 balls, during which Pakistan collapsed from 37 for 1 to 55 for 5, the Yorkshire bowler announced his authority. *Wisden* reported: 'His mixture of in-swingers, off-spinners and leg-cutters, his variation of pace and flight, bore the stamp of a highly skilled craftsman.' Denis Compton, in the evening of his career, also chose this occasion to play an innings which revived memories of his former grandeur. Compton's 278, his highest score in Test cricket, was a batting *tour-de-force*. He hit all but 27 out of 192 runs in partnership with Bailey.

Johnny Wardle joined Compton in another batting onslaught in the third Test at Manchester. Compton hit 93 out of England's first innings total of 359. Wardle rejoiced in an ideal situation for his big-hitting, striking three sixes and five fours in his 54.

Maqsood Ahmed was hit for two fours by Wardle and his replacement, the left-hander, Shujauddin fared even worse. Wardle hoisted two balls for six and then hit him straight for another six, the ball soaring over the sightscreen. Wardle's 50 came in 57 minutes and the runs were taken out of 75. 'He then began to swing his bat in a fashion which suggested that his interest in scoring had been satisfied and that he was prepared to turn his attention to the other side of the game,' commented the *Yorkshire Evening Post*.

Wardle's gleeful anticipation of a spinning feast was fully justified. Pakistan, in their reply, were always struggling against him and his new off-spinning partner, Jim McConnon. They were dismissed for 90 and the innings was over in three hours. *Wisden* sympathised with the distress of the Pakistan batsmen.

> Sometimes the ball flew from a length, at other times it squatted, and all the time the spin bowlers were able to make it turn sharply. Stronger sides than Pakistan would have been in trouble against the off-breaks of McConnon, who began his Test cricket with three wickets for 12 runs in six overs, the left-arm slows of Wardle, and the medium-pace cutters of Bedser.

Between lunch and stumps Pakistan lost 14 wickets for 155 runs.

Wardle and McConnon claimed most of the distinctions. Wardle took 5 wickets (4 for 19 in 24 overs and 1 for 9 in 7 overs) and McConnon 3 for 19 in 13 overs in the first innings. Wardle held two catches for McConnon, McConnon caught two for Wardle, one for himself and one for Bedser. In the follow-on Pakistan were harassed to the brink of defeat. Bedser was as menacing as Wardle, with whom he began the bowling.

In little more than half an hour four wickets fell for 10 runs. Wardle and Bedser were aided by a clutch of brilliant catches. At the close Pakistan were 25 for 4, still needing another 244 runs to make England bat again. They were rescued by rain; not another ball was bowled; and Wardle was left to lament another spoiled harvest.

Wardle, linking masterful spin and flight to secure seven wickets, had also to rue the folly of a rush for runs by England's senior batsmen at the Oval. England's target was only 168, and a superb 53 by Peter May seemed to have put the match firmly in their grasp. When May was dismissed England needed only 59 with seven wickets left. In a misguided attempt to win in a gallop Evans, Graveney and Compton all failed in a rash pursuit. On the last morning, as Godfrey Evans now relates, England looked to Wardle, the batsman, to salvage their honour. It was asking too much on a difficult wicket. Pakistan, with Fazal their acclaimed hero, speedily overwhelmed him. England lost their last four wickets for 12 runs.

Wardle, Appleyard and McConnon were the spinning choices for the MCC tour of Australia and New Zealand in the following winter. One of the ironies of the summer was that, after having been passed over for the tour, Laker and Lock suddenly found remarkable form. In their last ten championship games they took 103 wickets between them, Laker securing 59 and Lock 44, both for an average of less than nine runs apiece.

Wardle was by now regarded as a better prospect than Lock overseas; but Laker's omission was puzzling. That one of England's greatest bowlers of this or any other period should have to wait until his thirty-seventh year before gaining a place on an Australian tour – the 1958–9 series – was an affront to his talents.

There were few if any misgivings about Wardle's selection in Leonard Hutton's team in Australia. As Ian Peebles wrote:

> On the question of spin bowling there could be no doubt that when the time came to make a decision Wardle was ahead of all claimants. Lock at that time was under something of a cloud, his deadly faster ball virtually banned after his being no-balled in the West Indies, and his generally stock-in-trade slow mediums looking rather laboured. In the

West Indies, shorn of his destructive weapon, he had met with little success as a fast wicket bowler, which would be his sole function in Australia in an age of covered pitches. There is no reason to suppose that Australian umpires would be more charitable towards his action than their West Indian counterparts.

Peebles did, however, regret Lock's absence as a key fieldsman. 'It has made yet another gap in the superlative inner fielding ring which England had accumulated less than two years before.'

England's rousing victory in Australia was almost an exact replica of their success there more than twenty years earlier. Frank Tyson, as demoralising in his speed as Harold Larwood, and Brian Statham, playing a supporting role equal to that of Bill Voce, were a chilling combination. Larwood and Voce took 48 wickets at an average of 21.89 in 1932–3. In 1954–5 Tyson and Statham secured 46 wickets at 23.50 under Hutton's direction and leadership, which was just as rigorous, if not as controversial, as that of Douglas Jardine.

Johnny Wardle's crucial part in the triumph also closely paralleled the feats of his Yorkshire slow left-arm predecessor, Hedley Verity, on his first tour of Australia. Verity, like Wardle, had 'spelling' duties in Australia. His bowling figures in four Tests were 11 wickets at an average of 24.64 runs each. Wardle's wickets in the same number of Tests totalled 10 at a cost of 22.90 runs each. The comparison also extended to their release from the constraints of holding operations in the final Tests at Sydney in both series. Verity took 8 wickets for 95 runs, including five in the second innings. Wardle also demonstrated that the Australians were just as insecure against his unorthodox spin as pace when he secured 8 wickets at Sydney.

The sterling qualities of both Yorkshiremen in batting crises in Australia complete a happy coincidence of events. Arthur Morris, Australia's captain in the second Test at Sydney in December 1954, vividly recalls Wardle's aggression in that match.

> I blame Johnny – and blame is very much the operative word – for our loss at Sydney. On a green, moist and uneven wicket we were well on the way to a good first innings lead when Wardle came to the crease. He threw the bat at everything and was particularly severe on that great bowler, Bill Johnston.

Morris remembers Johnny's shattering impact on the Australian fieldsmen who cowered in positions not indicated in the fielding manual. At length he was forced to ask Johnston to take his sweater.

> Bill, however, begged for another over and it became sheer disaster.

Johnny hit him over the slips, over cover, over mid-on, everywhere but the places occupied by fielders. That innings lost us the initiative, lost us the Test match and, having been one up after the first Test at Brisbane, probably the series as well. Other players contributed to England's victory, but Johnny was the catalyst.

Wardle was top scorer with 35 out of 154 in England's first innings at Sydney. Nine wickets had fallen for 111 runs when he was joined by Statham in a fast and furious last wicket stand. Their partnership was the best of the innings. 'Wardle, who had not found the occasion too awe-inspiring for a little mild buffoonery, now let fly in earnest,' wrote Ian Peebles.

> He was especially hard on Johnston, off whom he took 18 runs in one over. Statham made a few crude and alarming strokes and a number of very good ones. The net result was that when the Australians woke up to the situation, 43 invaluable runs had been added.

Sir Leonard Hutton remembers how Johnny devised his own batting technique, a highly revolutionary affair, at Sydney. 'For four or five balls an over he failed to connect by anything between two inches and two feet. With others he did make contact and scored runs off them.' In a droll recollection Sir Leonard says Wardle had one particular shot which baffled the Australians.

> Johnny retreated towards the umpire and simultaneously advanced towards the bowler with his bat held aloft. He fooled them into thinking that a straight drive was his intention. In fact, the ball nearly always soared over the heads of the slips. All of this vastly amused the crowd.

Jim Swanton, on a more serious note, echoes the views of Morris and Hutton. 'Johnny had a very fine eye. He was a very dangerous hitter in the lower order.'

Wardle could not manage another act of piracy in the second innings. But Statham did, this time in company with Bob Appleyard. Despite a century by Peter May, who shared a fourth wicket stand of 116 with Cowdrey, England faltered against the new ball and lost 5 wickets for 28 runs. Lindwall took 3 wickets for 20 runs in 12 overs. Appleyard and Statham stepped calmly into the breach to add 46 runs in 50 minutes for the last wicket.

Neil Harvey, unbeaten on 92, played one of his finest innings for Australia at Sydney. He was the only batsman able to resist Tyson's searing pace. In one 50-minute spell Tyson took 4 wickets for 27 runs. His 6 wickets in Australia's second innings gave him 10 wickets in the match and England won by 38 runs.

Johnny Wardle played another vital innings of 38 – striking 16 off one over from the sorely tormented Johnston and another 14 in the next over from Johnson – in the third Test at Melbourne. Evans also hit out boldly and the pair added 46 in 40 minutes. According to John Arlott:

> There have been occasions when Wardle's runs were comedy: these were not. Only one of his hits was skied and that safely away from the field. In fact, he directed the ball with much skill, hitting Johnston square on both the on and the off.

Australia required 240 to win but they were overwhelmed by Tyson and Statham. By the last day they had reduced their target to 165 and had eight wickets intact. Appleyard and Wardle seemed to hold the key to an England victory on a worn pitch. Hutton did not have to resort to spin. *Wisden* reported: 'Sheer speed through the air coupled with the chance of a shooter at any moment left the Australian batsmen nonplussed. Tyson blazed through them like a bush fire.' In 79 minutes the match was over, the 8 remaining wickets falling for 36 runs. Tyson took 7 wickets for 27 runs and his figures on the last day revealed the full extent of the annihilation. They read: 6.3 overs, 16 runs and 6 wickets. Statham was the perfect accomplice, taking 2 for 19 and 7 wickets in the match as England won by 128 runs.

England kept their supporters on tenterhooks before resisting Keith Miller, bowling with characteristic fire, to win by five wickets at Adelaide. The retention of the Ashes cleared the stage for Wardle to spring into back-handed action in the final, rain-curtailed Test at Sydney. Exceptional downpours – the worst experienced in New South Wales for fifty years – held up play until two o'clock on the fourth day. Australia were all out for 221 in their first innings and followed on – 150 behind England's 371. Harassed and bewildered by Wardle's beguiling mixture of spinning allsorts, Australia ended the match 32 runs short and with only four wickets standing to narrowly avoid the indignity of an innings defeat in less than three days.

Wardle took 5 wickets in the first innings and 3 more when Australia batted again. He made his chinaman and googly turn prodigiously. Benaud was confounded by an off-break which spun grotesquely. Maddocks was so deep in despair that Evans threw back his head in disbelief when four times in one over the ball missed the stumps.

'The Australians' batting failed miserably against Wardle, who turned his off-breaks a considerable distance. He has found his true metier on Australian pitches,' commented Ian Peebles. Bill Bowes, watching his former Yorkshire colleague from the press box, was similarly impressed. 'My word, what a tangle these Australians were in against the wristy spinners of Wardle. I believe that Wardle, concentrating on this style of bowling, could keep his place in any side.'

While Surrey and Yorkshire grappled in an epic struggle for the county championship, Johnny Wardle and Tony Lock resumed their own personal battle for England recognition against South Africa in 1955. Wardle held sway in the first two Tests at Nottingham and Lord's. On a perfect wicket at Trent Bridge he bowled in his orthodox style to achieve a match return of 5 wickets for 57 runs in 61 overs, including 40 maidens. It was a performance of uncanny accuracy. The Yorkshire left-hander 'remorselessly played on the batsmen's nerves and patience,' commented one observer. In the South African first innings Wardle bowled 13 successive maiden overs, which included the wicket of McGlew. When Cheetham fell to a slip catch by Graveney off his bowling after lunch he had the remarkable figures of 8 overs, 7 maidens, 1 run and 2 wickets. His full return for the innings was 4 wickets for 24 runs in 32 overs.

Wardle's economy enabled Peter May to release Frank Tyson at his fastest on a pitch freshened by rain. Tyson's conquest of the Springboks in the second innings was as comprehensive as any of his feats in Australia. He secured his fiftieth Test wicket after only nine matches and took 6 for 28 in the innings. In his last spell he clean bowled Cheetham, Tayfield, Winslow and Adcock. He took 5 wickets for 5 runs in 7.3 overs. South Africa were all out for 148, beaten by an innings and five runs.

Peter May was no longer the caretaker captain at Lord's. He was appointed captain for the rest of the series after illness compelled Leonard Hutton to relinquish the leadership. May was not only sadly deprived of his England mentor; he also lost Tyson, his Nottingham matchwinner through injury. Tyson's replacement was Fred Trueman. Johnny Wardle had a new spinning partner, Fred Titmus, making his Test debut in place of the injured Appleyard.

Wardle took another 6 wickets in England's 71-run victory over South Africa at Lord's and seemed to have made his place safe for the rest of the series. Lock, the winner of the race to 100 wickets by early July, was restored to the England team at Manchester to the consternation of observers inside and outside Yorkshire. 'What mysterious "crime" has Johnny Wardle done – or not done – to warrant being replaced?' asked one astonished correspondent. Lock's selection meant that for the first time since the final Test against the West Indies at the Oval in 1933, there were no Yorkshiremen in the England team. Since the 1934–5 tour of the West Indies England had played in 114 Test matches at home and abroad and there had been at least one Yorkshireman – five in one Test against Australia in 1938 – in each of the Tests.

Johnny Wardle wryly commented: 'I was dropped for Old Trafford no doubt because they expected the wicket to take spin. Unfortunately, the weather was perfect and Lock took three wickets in the match in 71 overs for 144 runs.' Three South Africans, McGlew, Waite and Winslow scored centuries at Manchester. South Africa required 145 for victory in two and a quarter hours. They achieved the target, not without a few alarms, and won by three wickets with three minutes to spare in an exciting finish to a splendid contest.

Wardle, playing in his only Test at Leeds, and Lock shared the spinning duties in the fourth Test. Wardle bowled 66 overs for 133 runs and 5 wickets and Lock 38 overs for 108 runs and 2 wickets. England led South Africa by 20 runs on the first innings largely through Johnny's big-hitting. 'Wardle alone attacked the bowling,' reported *Wisden*. 'He helped himself to 24 from six strokes against Tayfield, including two drives for six into the top balcony of the football stand.'

McGlew and Goddard established a South African first wicket record in scoring 176 together in the second innings. Wardle and Lock were the perspiring, enduring duo in hot sunshine through the long hours of the South African innings. There was never a hint that they might falter; their rivalry, on this occasion, was committed to a common cause. 'There was a bowlers' delight on the bargain counter for the greater part of the first two days and with the first two innings completed the batsmen began to find satisfaction,' related Jim Kilburn.

Wardle's rewards on an arduous third day were the wickets of Goddard, McGlew, Keith and McLean. McLean was caught by Lowson at square-leg as South Africa attempted to force the pressure in the cool of the evening. Keith, playing a rustic pull shot, was bowled by Wardle. Johnny's spell after tea yielded figures of 3 wickets for 13 runs in 13 overs. Winslow, in an unavailing bid for quick runs, was dismissed by Statham. He fell to a catch created and taken by Lock in a sprawling dive. The catch, said one observer, was of such difficulty that it merited a touch of drama. Kilburn noted:

England maintained remarkable control over a threatening situation in the closing hours. Wardle bowled unchanged through the evening and though he was always experimenting in spin 18 overs cost only 25 runs and brought him three wickets.

South Africa drove home their advantage with a century by Endean on the Monday. Their subsequent victory by 224 runs produced criticism of Wardle for his indiscretions as a batsman. Trevor Bailey was last out after an innings of remarkable restraint. He scored eight runs in five minutes over two hours. He remembers his vain attempt to stave off defeat. 'I was trying to save the game but Johnny did not share my intention. He could be irritating as a man but I never expected him to do anything stupid as a cricketer.' In a situation requiring care and calm Wardle did not desert his attacking methods. He struck two fours and a six off Tayfield before being caught by Heine. 'Even the Yorkshire officials shook their heads in disapproval at Wardle's unrealistic outlook', commented one observer.

One Yorkshire enthusiast did, however, think the criticism of Wardle unwarranted.

> Thousands of spectators were filled with dismay at England's failure to accept South Africa's challenge of 366 in the last six hours, or rather dismayed not at the failure but at the manner of the failure. . . Right from the start of play the rate of scoring fell behind the clock and, as usual, the claims of spectators seeking due entertainment in return for their money (the Headingley receipts were £31,000) were counted as naught. South Africa, deprived of the services of Heine and, as it turned out, Adcock, were allowed to dictate the whole course of England's second innings. Perhaps Wardle should have batted with greater discretion – but, on the other hand, by this same method of 'chancing his arm' he obtained 74 runs for Yorkshire from the same attack at Sheffield. We did not get a spark of spirit from anyone except Wardle and we lost – deservedly so.

The circumstances were, of course, rather more desperate in a Test match which England were anxious not to lose; but the supporter was entitled to his indignation.

Wardle's days of supremacy over South Africa were still to come. In 1955 he had to look on again as Lock and Laker quelled the Springboks' fight-back in yet another tumble of wickets at the Oval.

# 7
# A Winning Message at Cape Town

*'Had the Wardle who bowled South Africa out at Newlands been on English television screens during his great hours he would have introduced millions to a type of bowling few have so much as seen. Wardle bowled it with rare accuracy and almost uncanny skill.'* – Charles Fortune, South African cricket commentator.

JOHNNY WARDLE discovered his cricket Eldorado on the South African veld. The riches of his bowling glittered brightly on the 1956–7 tour. This was his peak series in Test cricket and revealed his full prowess as a wrist-spinner. He took 26 wickets in the series at a cost of 13.80 runs each, and headed the tour averages with 90 wickets (105 in all matches) at 12.25 runs apiece.

At Cape Town, at the beginning of the New Year, he secured 7 wickets for 36 runs in the rout of the Springboks for 72. Louis Duffus, the veteran South African cricket writer, said: 'Wardle's unorthodox breaks were a constant source of bewilderment to all who played him.'

One South African newspaper report during the series was headed: 'Can't somebody do to Wardle what Taylor did to Barnes?' This was a reference to the feats of the legendary S. F. Barnes whose record of 49 wickets in four Tests at a cost of 10.93 runs each on the 1913–14 tour of South Africa is unsurpassed. Barnes took 17 wickets and 14 wickets in the Tests at Johannesburg and Durban. The English bowler, tall and erect as a guardsman, used his height to considerable advantage. Barnes relied more on his immaculate length and variations of spin than on deception of flight and pace. He had a fiery nature and was even more formidable when roused to a temper.

Carrying all before them and with Barnes almost unplayable, the MCC came to Natal. They lost the only game of the tour by four wickets. It was in this game that Barnes and Herby Taylor (the Natal and South African captain) fought one of the famous cricket duels. Natal needed 215 to win and Taylor, who had scored 91 in the first innings, followed this success with a century in the second innings. With Dave Nourse, Taylor put on 145 for the third wicket.

Taylor consistently 'farmed' the strike to shield Nourse from Barnes who eventually gave vent to his frustration. Throwing the ball down the wicket, Barnes, in this edited version of his anger, said: 'Taylor, Taylor, nothing but Taylor all the time. He won't let me get at that Nourse.' During the tea interval Johnny Douglas, the MCC captain, thinking to mollify his star bowler, asked whether a bottle of champagne could be purchased. Douglas was politely told that one could be obtained but not at the expense of the Natal Cricket Association.

Johnny Wardle's own triumphant progress was unimpeded in 1956–7. Doug Insole, the MCC vice-captain on that tour, believes that Johnny was at his happiest as a first-class cricketer during the series. Insole has a letter from Wardle, written after the tour, in which the Yorkshireman said that he had never enjoyed his cricket more than in South Africa. Before his great feat at Cape Town Wardle had taken 43 wickets in seven matches. Against Orange Free State at Bloemfontein in November he obtained 14 wickets in a day. Jim Swanton commented: 'One thing this match has emphasised beyond any doubt is the great value of Wardle.' The Bloemfontein wicket was flawless and yet, wrote Swanton, 'Wardle, exploiting all the arts of flight and spin, had 14 wickets for 96 runs in 25 overs. I wonder when any bowler on a plumb surface last had 14 wickets in a day.' Wardle was the spearhead in three victories gained by the MCC inside seven days' playing time.

All Wardle's England team-mates remember the beauty of his bowling in one of the most beautiful of cricket settings at Newlands, Cape Town. Johnny had every reason to be happy as he turned his off-breaks at sharply differing degrees. Wardle took his success calmly and quietly, said one writer, while regarding a letter from home as the most pleasant occurrence in his day. Back home Edna Wardle was rallying her husband with a non-stop supply of letters.

One of these cheering letters revived his flagging spirits at Cape Town. Johnny's response, veering on the ecstatic, demonstrates England's debt to Edna. In the following extract we are afforded a glimpse of her inspirational qualities.

Hotel Cecil,
Newlands,
Cape Province,

January 3rd, 1957.

Edna, You bugger, you have probably done more towards winning a Test match for England than any other woman before in the history of cricket. It is really fantastic that you could do so much for one man alone there on a cricket field.

I was dying for a letter from you this morning. I was up at 7.30 and ready at eight for it arriving but no letter. I went into breakfast and waited for the second lot of mail before I went to the ground which is fairly near. Still no letter. So I set off for the ground, feeling a little despondent.

Anyway, we took the field and eventually a few minutes before lunch Peter (May) put me on to bowl. I had felt all morning that I would get someone out but didn't like mentioning it. In the afternoon he gave me a few more overs and I took a wicket, one which we badly needed as well at the time.

We came off at tea and I was buggered. I felt like a shower, changing my boots and socks, etc., but still had the strength to look at the little table where they put the mail in the dressing-room. It is usually local stuff which naturally does not interest me . . . imagine my surprise and delight when I saw the 'message' (that's what the lads call it when there is a letter from you).

As soon as I saw it, I yelled out: 'This is it boys, we're all right now.' I completely forgot about my sore feet, the shower and changing my shirt. I just had time for a cold beer – your letter was that long and I only got through 12 of the pages before we were back on the field.

Well, I simply had to get back to finish it. Fortunately, the skipper took me at my word and put me straight on at the end I wanted. I was on top of the world and wouldn't have cared if Bradman or Hutton were batting.

I knew that I couldn't go wrong and took four wickets in next to no time. I was as strong as an ox. I did feel grand and lively and that, in itself, is a fair feat at 4.30 in this heat, after so long in the field. I finished with five for 53, in spite of a couple of dropped catches.

In South Africa's first innings Wardle broke the stand between Van Ryneveld and McLean, who had put on 47 for the fifth wicket. He also parted Endean and Waite who had added 52 for the seventh wicket. One observer said van Ryneveld and Endean were dismissed, padding up to balls which seemed almost capable of turning a corner.

Wardle, his stock enhanced as a matchwinner, had earlier betrayed tremors of anxiety that he might yet be supplanted by his spinning rival, Tony Lock, a fellow tourist in South Africa. 'Tony seems to be taking his exclusion very well,' he wrote in another letter before the surge of wickets at Cape Town ensured his retention by the selectors.

> He doesn't appear to hold anything against me. But possibly he had plenty of warning with past performances on this trip and was prepared to be left out. If they have missed Tony's fielding, it isn't because I have let them down. My ground fielding has been all right. But if I don't get wickets in this match (at Cape Town), I know I shall be out.

Doug Insole remembers how Lock accepted his demotion until the last Test at Port Elizabeth, when Wardle was injured, with very good grace. He believes that Lock and Wardle were closer to being friends in South Africa than at any other time in their joint careers.

England, in a series of slow over rates and snail-pace batting, did not bustle in the opening stages of the Cape Town Test. Tayfield, going on 50 minutes after the start of the match, bowled unchanged at one end, sending down 41 successive overs and taking 3 of the 4 England wickets which fell for 69 runs.

In another letter home Wardle related:

> Here I am again after watching our batsmen struggle all day on a perfect wicket for 214 runs. It is probably not a bad start but on such a good wicket it ought to have been tons better. The trouble is that they play carefully and then suddenly decide it's time to hit a four and get out to bad shots. Tayfield, the off-spinner, has bowled over 40 overs for 69 runs. I am convinced no-one can bowl that well on a wicket as good as this. Still there are signs of the wicket taking spin, so perhaps the longer we stay there the better chance I shall have with the ball. Our batsmen were thrilled to bits with today's performance. But they had to agree that had we fielded we would have been equally satisfied with that score.

Peter May, the England captain, took what one writer described as a 'circuitous route to victory' at Cape Town. May did not enforce the follow-on after South Africa trailed by 164 runs on the first innings. Alan Ross wrote:

> Throughout the day May adopted a defensive policy: he wanted the bowlers to get wickets, certainly, but he was not prepared to barter

any for time, and the field was set to guard against a bowler's errors rather than make the most of his successes. From the moment Wardle came on, it was plain that, with a score of 369 to bowl with, he was a more than fair insurance risk.

England extended their lead to 384, rightly in Wardle's view, to provide May with the incentive to persevere with Johnny's wrist-spin. Wardle recalled:

> South Africa needed nearly 400 to win and it was the first time under Hutton or May that I had been given the ball at the start of an innings. Peter realised that I was a matchwinner on that particular wicket. He spoilt it by asking me not to bowl the chinaman stuff at Trevor Goddard. I said: 'Look, skipper, let me bowl how I want to bowl, and I'll have him out in three overs. I'm not going to bowl orthodox to him. That would be just like giving him a net on this wicket. If I give him a net for half an hour, I'll struggle to get him out.'

Wardle's persistence won over the worried May. Johnny was allowed to bowl as he wished. 'I did Goddard, as I'd promised, in the middle of the third over, and from then on it was plain sailing.'

Johnny remembered the conditions in Cape Town as being ideal for his bowling.

> This wind was blowing – I was bowling the chinaman all the time then – and it kept drifting the ball out to the off. When it pitched it was spinning back quite a bit, especially when I hit Goddard's follow-through. Goddard used to bowl left-arm over and he had worn a patch about 18 inches outside the off-stump. When I pitched one there it did a tremendous amount. They couldn't pick one from the other.

South Africa resumed at 41 for two wickets on the last day. Wardle had dismissed McGlew and Keith on the previous evening. Defeat was inevitable but it came much quicker than expected. Eight wickets went down for 31 runs in an hour and a half. Four wickets fell at the same total, 67, and the last six South African wickets tumbled for five runs in 20 minutes.

Russell Endean recalls: 'We were aiming to defend and try to save the game. It was a hopeless situation and the circumstances were made for Wardle. But he gave a marvellous exhibition of bowling. He made the ball break by feet.' The former South African batsman describes his old England rival as a very shrewd bowler. 'Johnny knew when to bowl his wrist-spin. He didn't over-do it. He only used his unorthodox style when conditions were in his favour, or if there were plenty of runs on the board.'

Endean was given out 'handled ball' on appeal in South Africa's second innings. A ball from Laker spun from his pad outside the off-stump. It lifted gently straight above his head and might have fallen on his stumps had he not, his bat held limply by his side, chosen to divert it with his hand in a hockey-style manoeuvre. It completed a unique double. Endean, curiously, was also concerned in another unusual Test dismissal. He was the South African wicket-keeper when Hutton was given out 'obstructing the field' at the Oval in 1951. Hutton knocked a ball from Athol Rowan out of Endean's reach in trying to protect his wicket.

On the last morning at Cape Town Wardle was a swift and relentless executioner. His chinaman, as previously related, accounted for Goddard, who was caught by Bailey at slip; Waite was his next victim, bewildered by the googly, and Cowdrey accepted another slip catch; Watkins went to pull another googly and was caught off a hard return hit by Wardle; and Heine was bowled second ball by a straight, quicker delivery. Tayfield was missed first ball by May to deny Wardle a hat-trick. The England captain just failed to cling on to a fierce chance at mid-wicket. Three runs later Tayfield was given out, caught at the wicket, when Evans could have stumped him off the same ball but missed the bails as he whipped the ball across the wicket.

Wardle returned match figures of 12 wickets for 89 runs. England won by 312 runs and thus led 2–0 in the series after their first Test victory by 131 runs at Johannesburg. In the latter part of the Cape Town Test Wardle bowled almost exclusively chinamen and googlies and his control was remarkable. Wally Hammond, the former England captain, was an admiring onlooker. Hammond, who had tussled with the great Australian leg-spinners in the pre-war years, said it was the finest piece of spin bowling he had seen. Someone asked: 'What about Fleetwood-Smith?' Hammond replied: 'He left the Australian standing. I have never seen anyone with such control as a wrist-spinner.' Wardle listened to this conversation with mounting pleasure. 'I felt it was a wonderful feather in my cap to receive such a tribute,' he said.

The pitch was fairly worn at one end to which Wardle was bowling, commented one writer, and he was able to get the ball to break slowly. 'But he threw it well up and the batsmen, quite unable to fathom which way it would spin, pushed hopefully out. They were just good enough now and again to get a touch.' Godfrey Evans recalls: 'Johnny bowled magnificently. It wasn't a fast wicket at Cape Town. The ball did not come off all that quickly. If you could spin it – and Johnny could – and pitch it in the rough, the ball came off at varying heights, and often kept quite low.'

Doug Insole says that the great joy of Wardle's bowling on the tour was that quite often when the ball would not turn for the orthodox spinner, it would turn and bounce for the wrist-spinner. He recalls that he was obliged to leave the field on the last day of the Cape Town Test with a dose of what was euphemistically described as 'apricot fever'.

> Between excursions to the toilet, which were never sufficiently far apart to allow me to return to the field, I sat on the balcony with the South African team who were trying to guess, from a distance of 100 yards, which of John's deliveries was which. I remember one of them, John Watkins, who was a hell of a nice bloke, declaring himself to be absolutely certain of what was happening. I watched him go to the wicket and prove conclusively that he had no idea of what was going on. I was on hand when he returned to the hutch and had the good grace to admit that he was baffled.

Roy McLean was another of the Yorkshireman's perplexed adversaries in South Africa. 'Wardle tucks his hand away behind his right rump, wheels over his arm, and from the back of his palm, serves up a mixture of curves and spin that made a number of us look like junior school novices.'

McLean said that Godfrey Evans appeared most of the time to 'decipher Wardle's signwriting'. Evans says he always prided himself on his ability to 'read' the googly and the chinaman. In Kent he had learned his craft as wicket-keeper to Doug Wright, one of the fastest leg-spinners in the world. Wright was also a fine exponent of the googly, which he concealed very well.

> There was nothing more difficult than keeping to Doug on a dusty wicket. He was so quick with his looping action and he got a lot of bounce. You had to take the ball on its way up. Johnny, rather like Sobers in his slower style, gave the ball plenty of air. You usually knew whether it was the googly or not, but if you were uncertain it was possible to wait for the ball to pitch. This gave you enough time to anticipate the direction of the ball.

Evans' expertise contrasted sharply with that of Brian Taylor, his deputy on the tour. Taylor had spent most of the voyage out to South Africa tussling with Wardle's secrets. Even on arrival he was not always sure that he could detect the varieties of spin. 'If this 'keeper was baffled by Wardle's conjuring tricks, there must be some excuse for our batsmen,' commented Roy McLean.

Keith Andrew, with his wealth of experience against left-arm bowlers of varying styles, had considered himself certain to gain a place on the South African tour. He had been encouraged in this view by Taylor's unsuccessful attempts at keeping to the Northamptonshire left-hander, George Tribe, in a benefit match in the previous summer.

> Missing the South African trip was one of my biggest disappointments in cricket. I would have loved to have kept to Johnny at the height of his powers as a wrist-spinner. Brian spent hours on the ship deck, practising with Johnny, who tried to teach him how to pick his spin. But he couldn't keep to Johnny at all.

In the first twelve days of 1957 the MCC bowlers rejoiced in their supremacy. The haul of 58 wickets encompassed the whole range of South African cricket: a Test match, players from distant farming communities (the South African Country Districts XI at Queenstown, Cape Province), and a provincial eleven of reasonable strength (Border at East London). All were taken for an average of about 10 runs per wicket. Tyson had played only a small part in these successes and Laker had achieved only a modest share. The jinx bowler was Johnny Wardle. 'He had the South African batsmen, one and all, in a state not far removed from bewilderment,' related Charles Fortune. Wardle's figures at this stage of the tour were: overs – 226.2; maidens – 61; runs – 602; wickets – 60.

There was ample recompense, following a chastening defeat by a South African eleven at Pretoria, in the delightful tribute of a hero-worshipping local boy. The gushing compliment came when the train carrying the MCC team stopped at a village station during the journey to Durban. It reflected a wonderment undimmed by patriotism. Wardle's 10 wickets had been superseded by Tayfield's 12 in the match at Pretoria. Johnny and Trevor Bailey were immersed in a game of bridge when the boy suddenly appeared at the open window. He seemed anxious to communicate with Johnny.

'Sir, you're Mr Wardle, aren't you, sir? I saw you at Pretoria.' 'That's me, lad,' replied the preoccupied Johnny. 'Two hearts.' 'Mr Wardle, I think you're a wonderful bowler,' persisted the young fan. Johnny put down his cards and said: 'Hey, that's a grand thing to say. I'm reight pleased somebody appreciates me.' The boy responded: 'Oh, yes, Mr Wardle I was there at Pretoria every day, and I saw you take 10 wickets. It was marvellous.' One South

African companion of the two England players was prompted to rebuke the boy mildly for not favouring Tayfield in his praise.

'Oh, yes, Tayfield is good, but he's only half the bowler Mr Wardle is,' said the boy. An explanation was commanded. 'Well, Tayfield, he can only make the ball break one way. Mr Wardle can make it do anything: leg-break, off-break – just whatever he wants. You're wonderful, Mr Wardle, really you are.'

Johnny was now more than a little embarrassed at this torrent of idolatry. Trevor Bailey beamed with mischief. The young disciple waved vigorously at Wardle as the train pulled out of the station. Bailey leaned back in his seat and said, in a piping voice: 'Oh, Mr Wardle, you are wonderful.'

In his account of the Pretoria defeat by 38 runs, Wardle dwelt on the deteriorating conditions on a 'dust heap'. It was the first reverse suffered by an MCC side in South Africa since 1930–1. The game was played on a football ground and the pitch had only been laid for three months. It broke up on the first day and less than 500 runs were scored in the four innings. Wardle wrote:

> We aren't in a very good position at the moment. The South African side are over 100 in the lead and the wicket is getting steadily worse. The funny part about it is that Tony [Lock] didn't seem able to turn the ball at all on Saturday night. Everybody had expected him to waltz them out as fast as they came in.
>
> One end of the wicket is like our garden path. I had a bowl at that end after Tony had failed and managed to get a couple of wickets. Funston, who is 45 not out [the South African batsman scored 55 out of a second innings total of 116] was dropped off me by the wicket-keeper. When I hit a rough spot the ball simply ran along the ground but very slowly, so I wasn't particularly dangerous either. I reckon Jim Laker would have been the best bowler on this wicket but he isn't playing. Our batsmen will have to do better in the next knock, or we shall certainly lose.

Despite his reservations about his own bowling, Wardle took 6 wickets for 30 in the innings.

> I had a good spell this morning, taking four for seven, all of them clean bowled, three with the chinaman and one with the googly. I am afraid Tony didn't do so well but he was a little unlucky at times.

Lock had match figures of 5 wickets for 112 runs. Wardle explained: 'Tony's bad luck was that he was snicked for four so many times. He doesn't realise that if he bowled a bit slower the snicks wouldn't run so far. When they snick me it only results in one run, two at the most.' Jim Swanton, in his report on the match, put it even more succinctly. 'Lock, on a helpful wicket, sometimes pounces on the job with such ardour that he defeats himself.'

The MCC were set a target of 147 runs for victory. Wardle was promoted in the batting order in an attempt to wrest the initiative from Tayfield. As he related:

> The wicket isn't very good but we batted very badly again. After three fruitless swings at Tayfield, I decided I could stay there without too much worry. I did for two hours and scored 21. Then I was given out lbw. It was a very bad decision. I am certain I could have seen it through with Trevor (Bailey) and won this game. Anyway, I'm out and we're in a tangle.

Wardle thought the selection of three fast bowlers (Statham, Loader and Bailey) and the omission of Peter May was to blame for the MCC's defeat on a spinners' wicket and in a match not far short of Test status. He was also characteristically forthright in his condemnation of umpiring decisions which went against the team.

A report in the *Rand Daily Mail* during the match in Pretoria was headlined: 'MCC say sorry'. Wardle was among the players on both sides who had 'exchanged words they later regretted,' reported Jim Swanton. 'Peter May made it clear that he was not going to tolerate ill-manners on the field and this was the one and only lapse of its kind on the tour.' Johnny wrote in his private dispatch:

> I have just been detailed to go to the skipper's room at 10 o'clock. We have had a bit of excitement on the field and the umpires' decisions were a little queer. One chap was given not out lbw and he was absolutely plumb. When he got up to my end I heard him tell the umpire that he had played it. I know he didn't touch it and it annoyed me to hear him say this to make sure both their stories agreed.
>
> I called him a cheat in no uncertain terms because in a previous match he was twice caught by the wicket-keeper and refused to move until he was given out. When we were batting, Peter Richardson was given out and Doug Insole stood at the other end and ranted and raved with their captain and fielders for cheating.
>
> This has leaked out to the press and so no doubt we are being called in to be told to quieten down and not create any more incidents. I did not say anything to the umpire, only to the player concerned.

Wardle, Lock and Loader were the players on the carpet for swearing at the disciplinary meeting. They were strictly instructed that they must not, under any circumstances, misbehave again or the consequences would be severe. Johnny was suitably contrite at the meeting. He later reported: 'In my case it was only an isolated incident and I apologised to the batsman almost immediately afterwards. I shall have to make certain it doesn't happen again or my bonus will go for a burton.'

Freddie Brown, the MCC manager on the South African tour, today believes that Wardle, in his unorthodox style, might have clinched the series for England in the third Test at Durban.

> Peter May took him off after Funston, with some risky shots, had hit Johnny for three boundaries. It is easy to be wise after the event, but I think that if May had kept him bowling, he would have won the Test match for us. But it would have been a close thing as Wardle was tired after a long spell and was not bowling as accurately as before.

Peter May, a disconsolate figure as a Test batsman in South Africa, won the toss for the third successive time at Durban. It was his eleventh correct call in thirteen Tests as England captain. The omens for a conclusive victory seemed bright when Richardson and Bailey scored 103 runs together in the morning session. Bailey reached his 50 in two and a half hours, a brisk rate of progress by his standards. The opening stand was worth 115 when Richardson departed, lbw to Adcock for 68. May was also dismissed by Tayfield to continue his sequence of low Test scores (6–14–8–15–2). After he was out at three o'clock, England added only 33 runs in 26 eight-ball overs before the close of play. Tayfield bowled 14 consecutive maidens in the afternoon. Bailey scored 21 in three hours.

Jim Swanton confirms the widely held view that after the opening partnership the stage was set for England to press home their advantage on a perfect wicket. 'It was a ghastly innings by Bailey. He was a caricature of himself.' Swanton regards the sheet-anchor tactics of Bailey at Lord's, staying in to save a Test match against Australia, as admirable. But it was, he thought, a different matter when Bailey did not exploit a favourable position, with England on top at Durban.

Peter May makes another comment on the events of the first day at Durban.

> Trevor was an intelligent man who knew perfectly well what was wanted, but he was very limited and inclined to become bogged down technically and mentally by good bowling. I think that he saw himself as engaged in a personal duel with Tayfield and became so wrapped up in it that the momentum of the innings slipped away without him

realising it. It would have been nice to have been in a position to tell him to attack and not bother if he was out. But the rest of us were not doing well enough for that.

When bad light ended play 25 minutes early Bailey had batted for five and a half hours for 71. Indefensible batting had eroded England's advantage. At the close they were 184 for 4 wickets. Bailey's painstaking marathon seemed almost pardonable on the second morning. South Africa were in the ascendant. In 18 overs and three balls they took the last six England wickets for 34 runs. A fourth wicket stand of 59 runs between Goddard and McLean enabled them to finish the day only 78 runs behind, with six wickets left.

McLean went on to record his first century of the tour on his home ground against the Englishmen. It did not bear his usual aggressive stamp but it was marked by fine discipline and judgement. After their encouraging start, South Africa were restricted to a lead of 65 runs. Wardle, bowling mostly orthodox leg-breaks, took 5 wickets for 61 runs in 20 overs.

Insole's maiden Test century in England's second innings meant that South Africa required 190 to win in four hours and ten minutes. It was a scoring rate higher than either team had achieved in any previous innings in the series. Russell Endean believes that if England had had another 100 runs Peter May might have decided on all-out attack and won the match. South Africa, in fact, lost their first four wickets for 49 runs. Pithey was bowled second ball by Statham; Keith was caught by Lock (fielding substitute for the injured Bailey) off Laker. Wardle thereupon took the crucial wickets of Goddard, caught by Cowdrey, and McLean overthrown by his chinaman.

Endean and Funston, who offered a low, unaccepted return catch to Wardle, added 75 runs for the fifth wicket to give South Africa an outside chance of victory. As Endean relates:

> We were going for the target and living rather dangerously despite very slow over rates. But one or two catches were put down. May perhaps decided that rather than feed us with a few runs he could exert more pressure by putting other bowlers on. It was possibly a mistake because the wicket did suit Wardle's unorthodox deliveries. He must have fancied his chances.

May remembers that Tayfield had taken 8 for 69 in England's second innings without achieving great purchase for his spin.

I was not confident that we could bowl them out unless they took risks. In fact, South Africa never worked themselves into a position from which they looked likely to win. In the end, we were doing the attacking, and although we were not successful, a draw seemed not a bad thing in view of our 2–0 lead. In fact, it cost us the series.

At tea on the last day South Africa were 60 for 4, which showed them either disadvantaged by defensive tactics, or disinclined to risk another defeat. In two hours in the afternoon they added only 50 runs to fall well behind the clock. Wardle and Laker bowled 20 overs for 31 runs and 3 wickets. The hundred came up after three hours, and 90 runs were needed in the last 70 minutes. Funston and Endean were both dismissed at the same score, 124, but England had left it too late to force victory.

Johnny Wardle had no doubts that Peter May erred on the side of caution. He firmly believed that England squandered the chance to win the series at Durban. May would not allow him to bowl his chinaman and googly. 'I felt I could bowl them out with my wrist-spin. Peter preferred to keep them quiet and play for a draw. It didn't suit me at all.'

May's leadership, misguided or not, prevailed on this occasion; but Wardle was brave enough to defy the England captain when Roy McLean came to the wicket.

> I knew he would accept a challenge. I bowled this chinaman and, honestly, a lot of concentration went into it because I knew it was vitally important. I spun it like a top and Roy's eyes lit up when he saw it coming. I'd given it a nice bit of air and he rocked on his heels with a big backswing all ready to hit it for six. But the spin caused the ball to dip a little at the end of its flight. It turned about two feet and bowled him. Peter came dashing up from mid-on to congratulate me. I said to him: 'You won't be so pleased when I tell you what it was. I might as well tell you because if I don't someone else will. It were t'chinaman.' Peter replied: 'All right, but don't bowl it anymore.'

Wardle had to obey orders and exile his chinaman for the rest of the game. But, in one of our last conversations, he looked back with obvious dismay on a wasted opportunity. 'We should have slaughtered them. No, that's not quite right. But we should certainly have beaten them.'

Victory at Durban – the last Test played on the Kingsmead ground – would have placed the seal on his triumphs in South Africa. Alan Ross also reflected on the lack of enterprise by England.

After the fabulous events of the last six months, the proven economy as well as the destructive powers of Wardle and Laker, May ought not to feel that spin bowlers should be treated as delicately as Bristol glass. It is part of their scheme of things that the batsman should chance his arm against them, and they must be encouraged to keep the ball up, and to flirt with him, not discourage his attacking strokes as May required Wardle to do. Once Funston had taken 11 runs off three balls from Wardle, he made no bones about saving the match, rather than take any risk in winning it.

Hugh Tayfield, South Africa's match-winner with 19 wickets in the last two Tests at Johannesburg and Port Elizabeth, under-scored England's failure to gamble at Durban. Tayfield established a South African record of 37 wickets in a series, beating the 47-year-old record of Bert Vogler. For the second time in eighteen months South Africa had shown their powers of recovery – this time with greater reward – to tie the series against England. In 1955, they were also two down and rallied to level the series before losing at the Oval.

Johnny Wardle was, unhappily, unable to capitalise on a villainous wicket at Port Elizabeth in 1957. He would surely have revelled on a wicket where the improvising batsmen were as busy as moles trying to dig out the shooting deliveries. Two days before the match he slipped a cartilage in his left knee as he stepped down from a snooker table platform. It was a faintly ludicrous finale to his finest overseas tour. He was destined to play in only one more Test, against the West Indies at Lord's in the following summer.

# 8
# Furious Departure

> *'The tragedy of his dismissal was that we lost the most experienced player in the team, a man who knew more about bowling than any of us.'* – Bob Appleyard

JOHNNY WARDLE was on the rack of despair when he rashly discharged himself from first-class cricket in 1958. At thirty-five, he was a premier bowler at the peak of his career and esteemed for his cricket intelligence. It was a spectacular march into exile. The controversial series of articles in the *Daily Mail*, which he regretted almost as soon as they were printed, dwelt upon what he considered was a lamentable decision to appoint Ronnie Burnet as Yorkshire captain. Burnet, then in his fortieth year, had had no previous experience of first-class cricket although he had led Yorkshire's second eleven with distinction.

The MCC's subsequent withdrawal of their invitation to Wardle to tour Australia under the leadership of Peter May must rank as one of the most drastic actions ever taken against an established Test cricketer. A writer in *The Field* was only one of many to unleash the bumpers in a campaign of accusations and counter-accusations waged in the media. He wrote: 'The only respect in which Wardle's display of petulance, some of it possibly justified, differed from that of other well-known players in recent times was in the specificness of his charges and the virulence of his language.'

Some time after the publication of the articles Wardle was the speaker at a meeting at the Miners' Institute in South Elmsall, near Doncaster. One pitman, clearly displeased at the fall from grace of a revered South Yorkshireman, pointedly asked Johnny: 'Doesta think tha's been a fooil, Johnny?' His very direct question elicited the very direct reply: 'Aye, I have.'

Wardle's grievances, placed as they were in the full glare of publicity, inevitably courted disaster. They were a grave error of judgement, alienating many previously sympathetic supporters in Yorkshire and elsewhere, and even producing disaffection within his own family. Edna Wardle today remembers the sad episode and how she pleaded with her husband to cancel the articles.

> Johnny was terribly upset at the mounting criticism of him. He felt impelled to put his side of the case. He didn't realise what the consequences of his action would be. He had to let his anger out. I knew that his words – and they were well-intentioned and without thought of financial gain – would only make matters worse when they appeared in print.

The crux of the affair was that a domestic wrangle in Yorkshire had gained the dimensions of a national morality tale.

Wardle's public indictment of his captain, his views on the indiscipline of younger players and the ineptness of the committee and coaching staff, carried the taint of boorishness. Johnny's honour as a cricketer was severely bruised. One writer did, however, think Yorkshire's indignation was exaggerated.

> So far as his original misdemeanours are concerned, he is not the first player to believe that he could lead the side better than the appointed captain, nor is he the only one to give vent to frustrated feelings by swearing on the field. But these are venial sins, and it would be a namby-pamby world in which they were too harshly punished.

Jim Laker thought that the Yorkshire decision to dismiss Wardle was a panic measure. He considered it a slight on the MCC selectors and that it inferred that Yorkshire set a higher standard of conduct and team spirit than the MCC. 'Surely if Yorkshire wanted to do without Wardle they should have waited until he came home from Australia.'

The original announcement of Wardle's dismissal, to take effect at the end of the year, was made by Yorkshire on 30 July, three days after his selection to tour Australia and New Zealand. It came in a terse statement by the Yorkshire secretary, John Nash, during the game against Somerset at Bramall Lane, Sheffield. Nash said: 'The Yorkshire committee have informed J. H. Wardle that they will not be calling on his services after the end of the season.'

The dismissal, together with the departures of Bob Appleyard and Frank Lowson a short time earlier and the move by Willie Watson to Leicestershire at the end of the 1957 season, meant that Yorkshire had released four England players in less than twelve months. The explanation offered by the Yorkshire committee was that team rebuilding was the sole reason for dispensing with older players. Brian Sellers, the former Yorkshire captain, was a member of both the Yorkshire and MCC committees. He said that Wardle's dismissal was a lightning decision and had not been discussed before the Sheffield meeting. He maintained that he was unaware of the move when he and his fellow MCC selectors had named Wardle as a member of the touring party.

Asked how he reconciled Wardle's selection for England with the Yorkshire announcement, he said: 'They are two different things. Wardle may be good enough for England but not for Yorkshire.' Sellers was ever forthright in his county allegiance. In his order of priorities Yorkshire always came first. It explains his curt response to the questioning reporter.

Even more significant, in conveying the justice or injustice of the sacking, it offers a telling pointer to the division of views on Wardle's personality traits as an England and Yorkshire player. Jim Swanton, who travelled with the Yorkshireman on three overseas tours, is quick to emphasise that he never saw or heard of any misbehaviour by Wardle on or off the field. Swanton accepts that the situation in Yorkshire was plainly different, though he believes that Wardle was far from being the only culprit in a highly competitive camp.

Another man rallying to Wardle's defence is Keith Andrew, currently the National Cricket Association's chief executive at Lord's. Andrew remembers, with gratitude, Wardle's friendship on the 1954–5 tour of Australia. 'I think there must have been some insensitive people around if they couldn't get the best out of Johnny. They can't have been trying too hard.'

The clamour of criticism which followed Wardle's dismissal in July 1958 raged with the ferocity of a forest fire during the following month. The discontent had, however, flickered throughout the summer. Resentment grew in the Yorkshire dressing-room at the tactical deficiencies of Ronnie Burnet. Johnny Wardle, as senior professional, was not alone in his view that the team was 'carrying the captain'. Brian Close says:

> We were beginning to look a bad side in 1958. The committee had asked Johnny to look after Ronnie. He tried to offer advice about changing bowlers and field placings and did his best to help. But there came a period when Ronnie did not take too much notice of Johnny and inevitably there was a blow-up.

Close remembers the final confrontation between Burnet and

Wardle during the lunch interval in the match against Somerset at Sheffield. The inference of Burnet's words was that Johnny was not trying.

> I thought Ronnie must be joking. Even if Johnny had hated his captain he would never have gone on to the field and not tried. Johnny was a 100 per cent Yorkshireman.

Burnet's charge was too insulting for Wardle to ignore. Close continues:

> Johnny was instantly on the offensive. He was never one to be shy if the circumstances demanded it. He rounded on Ronnie and said: 'At the beginning of the season I was asked to give you advice. You've taken no bloody notice and, as a result, you are making us professionals look idiots out there.'

The late Bill Bowes, in his recollections of a troubled season, took a different stance.

> The Yorkshire committee wanted Johnny to help bring on the youngsters. He couldn't do it. He wanted to bowl at both ends and get all the runs. He should have been a good influence on the side as one of our most knowledgeable cricketers. Johnny was not as helpful as we hoped he would be.

Wardle's catalogue of complaints, vehemently paraded in the national press, included younger Yorkshire players among the targets of his anger. As senior professional, he had strongly urged the imposition of an 11pm curfew for all players during matches. Pursuing his claim of indiscipline in the team, Wardle said:

> It is an elementary point that to be fit to play cricket you have to get to bed at a reasonable hour. I have known some Yorkshire players come back to the team's hotel during away matches at times varying between midnight and 1am. [Other observers clocked the revellers in at an even later hour.] When I saw these same men drop catches the next day it was small wonder that I got mad. Maybe I swore with justification.

Bill Sutcliffe does not agree that the progress of the county's young men in the 1950s was imperilled by Wardle's rigorous professionalism. Sutcliffe, as captain, remembers the complaints relayed to him by the kindly Cyril Turner, a member of Yorkshire's championship side of the 1930s.

I never took the complaints any further. My view was that if you are playing for Yorkshire you shouldn't be half asleep and dropping catches. I told Cyril: 'It won't do these lads any harm to get a rollicking. It's all part of their Yorkshire upbringing.'

Sutcliffe stoutly maintains that Wardle was no different in his attitudes to the pre-war Yorkshire players with whom he was brought up as a boy. 'I know they wouldn't have put up with second-rate fielding.' He adds: 'The moans about Johnny playing pop with the lads were really just an excuse for lapses in form. If they'd grumbled in father's time, they would have been told to shut up.'

Bob Appleyard endorses Sutcliffe's assessment of the situation.

Johnny was keenly competitive. He had been brought up in a hard school and he was rightly scathing of inattentive colleagues. It was a tough environment we were performing in and the boys should have learned from his attitudes to the game.

Appleyard remembers the strict regime of his days as an engineering apprentice.

At work you were told what to do and you wouldn't be told a second time. There could be no mistakes after that. It was the same in cricket. If you dropped a catch or conceded a boundary unnecessarily, you were surrendering the initiative to the opposition.

Bob Platt, a younger member of the Yorkshire team in the 1950s, says Johnny's method of helping the youngsters was to kick them up the backside.

A picture of Wardle as a cricketer flawed by a mean streak is portrayed by Raymond Illingworth, one of the Yorkshire youngsters stung by the fury of Johnny's tongue. Illingworth recalls:

When I first started in the Yorkshire side, the lads were frightened to death to go for a catch off his bowling because of his temper. I dropped a catch and he argued with me. I had a real blow-out with him and it cleared the air. I then caught everything off his bowling.

Wardle, even in the eyes of his admirers and there were none who doubted his integrity as a cricketer, could be crushing in his criticism. Timidity in a fellow professional almost seemed to fuel his anger. Illingworth says if you sensibly stood your ground in any argument, you would gain his respect. 'I got on better with Johnny than most of the players. He was always punctual and well-dressed and he helped me a lot in the nets and in matches.'

At the end of one game against Gloucestershire at Cheltenham Wardle took Illingworth out to the wicket. 'I had bowled well in the match, but Johnny explained how I could have improved on my performance. He showed me where he had pitched the ball and compared his direction with mine.' In another match at Edgbaston Wardle fielded at mid-off to Illingworth's bowling. 'He kept saying: "Concentrate!" At the end of my spell, he said: "You've had your lesson and I won't stand at mid-off again." '

Brian Close, with characteristic pugnacity, did not pull his punches in one quarrel with Wardle at Dover. None were actually exchanged, but Close believes that one of the flaws of the Yorkshire leadership was not taking a strong line, as he did, in such a situation. Conversely his own choice for the Yorkshire captaincy would have been Wardle because of Johnny's strength of character.

> He was not a man to watch fellow players taking cricket light-heartedly. Johnny was interested in winning matches. He hated losing and most of all he hated losing matches which could be won. He would have ensured that the Yorkshire team was a 100 per cent workable outfit.

On the vexed issue of dropped catches, Close says that Wardle was not alone in his displeasure. Other Yorkshire bowlers, Trueman and Appleyard among them, would fret and curse if catches went astray. 'Fortunately for me I used to take more impossible catches than the others.'

Mike Cowan, as another younger player, was reportedly reduced to tears by Wardle's petulance. If this was indeed the case, he masks the anguish of his youth in a remarkable manner. 'I don't think I was a bad kid, and Johnny seemed to take a shine to me. It was all a new world to me, difficult to absorb, but you couldn't help being impressed with what Johnny did as a cricketer.'

Cowan and Wardle travelled to Lord's together for the traditional opening fixture against the MCC. 'It was my first match for Yorkshire. I took four wickets, including a return catch off Nigel Howard. At the end of the over Johnny strode towards me. I thought he was going to say: "Well bowled".' Wardle's response was intended to subdue Cowan's pardonable elation. 'If you'd missed it,' said Johnny, 'you'd have swallowed it with your mouth open like that.'

Cowan is now able to relate with equanimity the sitter he dropped off Kent batsman, Jack Pettiford, at Maidstone in 1958. As a popular after-dinner speaker today, it is a story of shame in his repertoire, a fragment of apologetic recall designed to chide himself, not Wardle.

> I was fielding at mid-off and Johnny had tried for three overs to lure Pettiford into making a mistake. Sure enough he held one back and Jack played too soon. He dollied up a gentle catch, not very high, and it hit me on the chest. I dropped it. I was very embarrassed and fearful. My immediate reaction was: 'God, I'm in for it now.' Then I heard this voice saying: 'Don't worry lad.' I thought this rather strange coming from Johnny. I expected him to read the riot act. Instead he simply said: 'It was my bloody fault for putting you there.'

The note of sarcasm was probably more unnerving or menacing than an outburst of undisguised abuse. A more charitable interpretation would be that Wardle was issuing an ultimatum to Cowan to concentrate his mind. If he wanted to succeed with Yorkshire, there was no time for day-dreams.

Geoff Cope was one of the later school of Yorkshire cricketers who benefited from Wardle's wisdom. He shares Brian Close's view that Wardle was one of the few senior professionals of the time to give freely of his advice to young players. 'The older players that I knew, who were kids in Wardle's time, said you would get a rollicking if you misfielded or dropped a catch. But he was always the one whose hotel bedroom door was open at night if you wanted to sort out a problem.'

Cope thinks it quite possible that people were upset by Wardle's candour. In higher circles Johnny suffered for being so forthright. He believes that Wardle warranted special consideration because of his professional attributes and that his constructive criticism, however roughly conveyed, had to be carefully digested.

It is salutary to glean the impressions of a younger cricketer, even if he was only a boy during Wardle's violent tussle with the Yorkshire hierarchy in 1958. Cope, as an off-spinner banned for 'throwing' in the 1970s, suffered his own heartaches. Wardle was the man deputed to act as his bowling tutor. Their friendship during this time blossomed into a father-and-son relationship. In their many conversations during his own trauma, Cope began to appreciate the frustration of Wardle all those years ago.

> I know the kids thought the world of Ronnie Burnet. He had done a super job with the second eleven. But he could not adopt the same measures in the first team.

As an example, Cope cites Wardle's lessons in patience as a bowler and his philosophy in the following words:

There is the batter at one end whom you would rather not stay too long. You have got the ball and it is up to you to dictate to him how long he remains at the crease. You work and work away and then the batter makes a mistake. And someone drops it. Just imagine Johnny's horror.

Johnny's view was that you did not get the fielders, particularly the 'batting' fielders who thought like a bowler. His way of playing pop was to stress how much work and thought, perhaps over an hour or more, had gone into tying a batsman down.

One vital lesson passed on by Wardle is firmly fixed in Cope's memory. 'Johnny said: "You've always got to educate the rest of the lads in the dressing-room as to the way you, as a bowler, are thinking." '

Wardle's teachings were tossed aside by Yorkshire in a furore over manners in a bitter and tragic climax to his career. He was branded as a trouble-maker and as a major source of the disunity existing in the Yorkshire dressing-room. Bob Platt remembers the comment of a neutral observer, a southern captain, on the dissension: 'You've got a bad dressing-room up there. Wardle is a very hard cricketer, but he is not the one who causes the problems.'

On 12 August 1958, after a two-hour meeting at Bradford, Yorkshire announced that Wardle's engagement would be terminated forthwith, because he had broken his contract by writing, without permission, the articles in the *Daily Mail*. Wardle, the committee stated, had been warned several times about his conduct on and off the field. There had been no improvement and it had been decided to dispense with his services. The allegations are strongly disputed by Edna Wardle and the evidence from other less impartial witnesses is inconclusive.

Norman Yardley was a member of the Yorkshire committee which took the decision. In retrospect, he is inclined to the view that the move to dismiss Wardle was unduly precipitate. Under his captaincy Wardle had been perfectly manageable and an admirable colleague except for occasional tantrums. He explains that, unlike today, Yorkshire did not then offer contracts. One of the rules of the club was that players had to be given notice by the end of July so that they could make arrangements for the following season. Yardley believes that if the present situation of renewal of contracts at the end of the year had applied in 1958, the trouble might have been averted.

Basil Robinson, brother of Ellis Robinson, the former Yorkshire off-spinner, remembers Wardle's distress after receiving the news of his dismissal in the Somerset match at Sheffield. Robinson recalls: 'I was sitting upstairs in the pavilion with Maurice Tremlett. Maurice asked me to stay on and have some tea with him.' Basil was unable to accept the invitation because he had arranged to meet friends at the interval.

> As I went down to rejoin my pals for a drink, Johnny was just coming out of the Yorkshire stripping room. Johnny said: 'Do me a favour, Basil, walk down with me and keep talking. I've just got the sack and all the press are waiting for me.' I took him down past the long bar at Bramall Lane to the car park and put him in his car.

Wardle was grief-stricken, his face ashen with despair. He mumbled a word of thanks to Robinson. Basil says: 'Johnny was on the brink of tears.'

Wardle remembered seeking out the Yorkshire club chairman, Clifford Hesketh, after his dismissal. He told Hesketh: 'After all the years I have given to Yorkshire cricket why couldn't you give me the chance to resign?' Hesketh said that his, Wardle's, case had been considered at the same time as the decisions on Frank Lowson and Bob Appleyard, who had been previously released by Yorkshire. 'We could not decide about you at that time,' he said.

Hesketh then accused Johnny of not treating the younger members of the side properly, and that he had the wrong attitude altogether for a senior professional. 'I stood quite still while he told me that when I was taking wickets I was all right,' recalled Wardle. 'But,' continued the Yorkshire chairman, 'as soon as you have to struggle for them and things don't go your way, you start swearing on the field. What is more you have generally lost interest to such an extent that you will bowl long hops just to be taken off.'

Hesketh's words were read from a prepared statement. The next charge was that Wardle had said: 'Yorkshire are only a team of lads. Why should I bother?' Wardle said that he challenged the chairman to produce the man who had made this accusation. The charge was withdrawn. At the end of their brief meeting Wardle knew that the axe had fallen. 'I was a naughty boy of the first order.'

Charlie Lee shares the view of many observers that there was a certain inevitability about the events leading to Wardle's sacking. Lee wonders if a wise counsellor within Yorkshire's ranks might have checked Wardle's indiscretions.

> You could not guarantee that Johnny would have taken any notice. He was always his own man. But someone ought to have said to Wardle: 'Now look, with all this chuntering, there will be those people

who might think you are setting yourself up against the club. If that is the case, you have no chance. The club, in the final analysis, must always come first before any individual, however talented.'

The concluding argument, which Lee believes might have saved the day, would have been to say to Wardle:

> If you play your cards right, which does not mean compromising your integrity, only a foot on the brake, there is every possibility you *might* take over from Ronnie Burnet very soon. He is not going to be here for long. You could have a second benefit and end up with over 3,000 wickets.

Ellis Robinson thinks his old friend overplayed his hand. 'He should have had the intelligence to know that you cannot buck the Yorkshire system. Other people before him had tried and lost the battle.'

Bill Sutcliffe also believes that calmer influences should have prevailed. His wry assessment is that Wardle was sacked because he wanted to uphold the standards of Yorkshire cricket. Sutcliffe is in accord with those who say that Ronnie Burnet was not quite good enough as a cricketer to captain Yorkshire. 'Where Johnny made his mistake was that Ronnie did not pretend to be. In these circumstances, Johnny should have been more tolerant.' Sutcliffe says that if he had remained as Yorkshire captain he would have defended Wardle.

> I would not have allowed the committee to ride roughshod over him. We would have gone before the committee and all the facts would have been brought out into the open before the crisis had a chance to develop. Had that happened, Johnny, who loved playing cricket for Yorkshire, would have responded in a proper manner.

Bob Appleyard also looks back with sympathy for Wardle in the controversy.

> The tragedy of his dismissal was that we lost the most experienced player in the team, a man who knew more about bowling than any of us. He was the one who could have done most to maintain Yorkshire's spinning tradition. In the short term it did not matter because Ronnie's boys did well. In the long term, however, Johnny's departure had immense repercussions for Yorkshire cricket.

The sequel to the Yorkshire announcement was that the MCC, who had initially refused to be drawn into a domestic matter, called a special meeting of their full committee. It has since been implied that strong pressure was exerted in the Yorkshire report to the MCC to omit Wardle from the Australian tour. Wardle attended the meeting chaired by the MCC president, the Duke of Norfolk, at Lord's on 19 August. Edna Wardle recalls the high drama of the meeting and Peter May's dejection after hearing the news of Johnny's dismissal from the MCC party. May himself says it was a very sad day. 'It was a great loss for me as captain. I was disappointed that Johnny would not be available for the tour.'

Edna Wardle remembers that her husband was asked if he had read the offending articles before publication. 'If he had answered in the negative, he would, I think, have gone to Australia.' Johnny could not give this assurance. He told the MCC jury: 'Yes, I did.'

Ronald Aird, the MCC secretary, pronounced the verdict of his committee. 'I am sorry Johnny, you're out.' Wardle stood erectly to attention. His apology was measured and restricted to one rueful sentence: 'It is my fault, and I asked for it.'

There was a revealing postscript to the affair, amid the rejoicings at Scarborough after Yorkshire had won the championship in 1959. Bob Platt and Fred Trueman were enjoying a celebration lunch when a county member walked up to their table to congratulate them on the triumph. 'They've all done well,' said Fred. 'But if we'd had Wardle in the team, we'd have won the title by the middle of August.'

# 9
# Burnet on Wardle

> *'What happened was an absolute tragedy. He should have played for Yorkshire for another 10 years.' – Ronnie Burnet.*

TWELVE months after the sad saga of enmity Ronnie Burnet was hailed as Yorkshire's saviour after leading a team of innocents to the county's first outright championship for 13 years. The *Yorkshire Post* enthused:

> Oh what a beautiful morning! The cricket championship has come to Yorkshire and we cannot forbear to salute what at the season's outset had seemed an unlikely championship side. But the pennant has been taken away from Surrey with the sheer will to win . . . not for many seasons has there been such sporting cricket.

In October 1959, Burnet and Wardle met for the first time since their dispute, at a dinner in Doncaster. 'Johnny walked across the floor to greet me and said: "Congratulations, skipper. Well done." ' The Yorkshire captain replied: 'You should have been with us when we did it.' Wardle's response was a mixture of self-rebuke and amazement. 'I know I should. I'm sorry. I didn't think you could do it.' Burnet today believes that it was a sincere expression of regret and a confirmation of Wardle's view of him.

Ronnie Burnet has for the first time broken his silence to chronicle a feud which, he insists, was not of his making. He emphasises that he was never at any time anti-Wardle and made strenuous attempts to achieve a rapport with Johnny, even to the point of over-ruling the Yorkshire committee on the choice of senior professional. Burnet says he was urged by the committee to give Vic Wilson the job. He was warned that Wardle was a disruptive influence. Burnet declared that the post was Wardle's by right and that he would be in an invidious position if he gave it to someone else. 'He must be given the chance to do it, and if he performs his duties correctly, we shall have no bother,' he told the Yorkshire committee.

Burnet's elevation to the Yorkshire captaincy after more than twenty years as an amateur in the Bradford League fulfilled the long-held ambition of his father. It was a gamble to thrust a man without first-class experience into such an onerous position, even if only as a caretaker leader. But the move was prompted by Burnet's disciplinary qualities and his success as Baildon skipper and later in leading Yorkshire's second eleven to the Minor Counties title in 1957.

In 1949, Baildon, under his captaincy, won the Bradford League Second Division. They were also First Division champions for three years in the early 1950s and won four league cup trophies during this period. Burnet took over the Yorkshire second eleven captaincy from Michael Crawford in 1953. From that time until he succeeded Bill Sutcliffe as first team captain in 1958 he fostered the talents of such players as Brian Stott, Ken Taylor, Jackie Birkinshaw, Don Wilson, Phil Sharpe, Bob Platt and Mel Ryan.

All of these youngsters, who were to become the nucleus of the championship winning side in 1959, responded well to his leadership and found him a likeable personality. Don Wilson, as Yorkshire's new slow left-arm bowler, was the direct beneficiary of Wardle's dismissal. Wilson, who today enjoys a considerable reputation as the MCC's head coach at Lord's, gives Burnet the highest possible rating as captain. Others, like Bob Platt, concede that Burnet made Yorkshire 'happy again', but believe that he was unfitted as a cricketer to lead a team of seasoned professionals.

As Yorkshire's second eleven captain, Burnet had sent many players up into the first team. He was dismayed by the reports he received from them of the bad spirit in the side. The Yorkshire seniors were considered by many to be a group of prima donnas. Wardle was tagged as the major culprit. He was condemned as an unpleasant man, unhelpful to the boys whom he abused at all times.

Ted Lester was senior professional to Burnet in the second eleven in 1956. He believes that his appointment was partly designed to direct his captain on the greater problems of first-class cricket. Lester was and is a fervent admirer of Wardle's gifts as a bowler. Their friendship – a close one – was forged as young Yorkshire cricketers after the war. He was therefore eminently qualified to make the judgement that Johnny could pose difficulties unless he was strongly handled.

Before taking over the reins of the Yorkshire captaincy in 1958 Burnet had a series of meetings with Wardle during the preceding winter. The exchanges, designed to establish a good working relationship, were courteous but Burnet says he felt an undercurrent of resentment that he had been given the job. 'I think Johnny was disappointed at not getting it himself. His general attitude was: "We're used to doing it. We'll get on with our tasks." '

Burnet accepts that Wardle's resentment stemmed from the fact that he did not think his captain was worth a place in the team. On playing terms he does not disagree with this verdict. 'But I was given a mandate *not* to sort Wardle out but to sort Yorkshire out and get the team to work together.'

At first it seemed that the miscast characters were to embark on a tolerably smooth voyage together. Their ship was blown off course when Burnet was injured in a match against Cambridge University at Fenners, early in the 1958 season. He was out of the side for six weeks. Wardle, relishing his role as acting captain, clearly found it difficult to revert to being a subordinate when Burnet was restored to fitness.

The first outward signs of Wardle's disenchantment came in the match against Derbyshire at Chesterfield in early July. Burnet remembers how a thunderstorm on the previous night had delivered a sticky wicket to the Yorkshire bowlers.

> The temperature was around 80 degrees, it was steaming hot, and we had ideal bowling conditions. After a few overs from Platt and Cowan, I got Wardle and Illingworth on. Arnold Hamer (in his benefit match) and Charlie Lee, both Yorkshiremen, were the opening batsmen. Now, Johnny was bowling superbly, and so well that they couldn't lay a bat on him. The 'playing and missing' went on for about 45 minutes.

Burnet's reaction was to offer, as he puts it, a polite request to Wardle to strive for a fuller length.

> I took the ball up to Johnny and said: 'You are bowling marvellously, but you are beating the bat by at least a foot. Why don't you try pitching the ball further up? They will think they can get to it and you will make contact. They haven't a price of scoring runs, but you will get an edge.' This was all said in the nicest possible way. But in a loud voice that could be heard all round the ground, Johnny replied: 'I've been playing this game for 12 years and you come in and tell me how to bowl. You must be wrong in your head.'

A shower of expletives punctuated the response. Burnet switched Wardle to the other less responsive end to show him the error of his ways. He says that Wardle then proceeded to bowl an over of long hops. 'Five of them were hooked for four and, if it hadn't been for a diving stop by Doug Padgett at deep square-leg, it would have been six.'

Burnet promptly ordered Wardle to take his sweater and go down to field at fine leg. 'I played without him as a bowler. But I made a big mistake. I should have sent him off the field.' The expulsion of his senior bowler to the outfield seems warranted, but the statistics of the Derbyshire innings are at variance with Burnet's account. Wardle bowled 40 overs for 71 runs and 3 wickets; Illingworth bowled 29 overs for 50 runs and 3 wickets; Close 12 overs for 30 runs and 3 wickets. In his farewell season, soured by mutiny towards his captain and ending in disgrace at the end of July, Wardle secured 91 wickets at a cost of 15.39 runs each.

The figures show that his prowess as a bowler remained undiminished. That he could be wayward as a man and singleminded as a bowler does show some resilience in the prevailing acrimony. The rift between Burnet and Wardle perceptibly widened after the events at Chesterfield. Any question of co-operation between the two men had disappeared. Burnet found himself increasingly appalled at the spate of dropped catches, occasioned, he says, by Wardle's violent behaviour. Mike Cowan, in particular, was so frightened that he dropped five in succession through sheer nervousness.

Cowan's unease was mercilessly disregarded in the well-documented mishap against Kent at Maidstone. Wardle's displeasure, and his manner of showing it, convinced Burnet that he could no longer tolerate the disharmony. In his account of the incident, Burnet recalls:

> We caught Kent on another sticky wicket. Johnny was bowling with great control in his orthodox style. He only needed two fieldsmen on the onside – a mid-wicket and a deep mid-on. He personally took Cowan out of the offside field and put him at mid-on. Inevitably, one of the late order batsmen played a cross-bat shot at Johnny. The ball went up in a gentle arc to Mike. He went pale again. He didn't touch it; the ball hit him on the breastbone, and went to the ground.

Burnet was fielding at mid-off and at the end of the over he made a point of walking across with Wardle to avoid a confrontation with Cowan.

We didn't say a word as we moved towards Mike. Mike stuttered an apology. 'I'm terribly sorry, Johnny, I didn't mean to drop it.' Johnny put his hands on Mike's shoulders and said: 'It's all right, Mike, don't worry.' He then edged his face nearer and said: 'It's my fault for putting you there.' All the players heard the remark and they were disgusted at Johnny's conduct.

Newspaper placards on the journey from Maidstone to London did nothing to allay Burnet's anger at the situation. They announced the sackings of Appleyard and Lowson. Burnet had not been consulted about these developments. On the following day at the Oval he met Clifford Hesketh, the Yorkshire chairman, and told him:

> My opinion should have been sought. I am captain of the side. Had I been consulted I would have included a third player – Johnny Wardle. As long as we have him in the side we shall never have any team spirit. I want you to call a meeting at Sheffield and I will put the full facts before the committee.

The lunchtime meeting took place during the match against Somerset and Burnet officially recommended the dismissal of Wardle. Afterwards John Nash, the secretary, stepped into the Yorkshire dressing-room and handed a note without comment to Wardle. There was a moment of fraught silence and then, to the consternation of the rest of the team, Johnny said: 'Bloody hell, I've been sacked.' Wardle threw the paper on the floor and pointed an accusing finger at Burnet as he swept out of the room. 'He knows all about it. Ask him.'

The sombre headlines next morning, carrying the news of the abrupt dismissal of an idolised cricketer on his home ground at Sheffield, brought a rush of popular support for Wardle. He was cheered to the echo and Burnet was booed just as vociferously by the spectators milling on the terraces. Philip Sharpe had scored a majestic first century for Yorkshire on the opening day and the stage was set for Wardle to put Somerset to rout. A burden had been lifted from his shoulders and his bowling arm swung with a fearful vengeance. He took 6 wickets for 46 runs in 33 overs and 2 more as Trueman's ally in the second innings as Yorkshire won by an innings and 84 runs. Burnet recalls: 'He was a different bowler after he was sacked. He didn't bowl a loose ball. He was magnificent, frighteningly good, much more so than he had been all season. It was incredible.'

The mood of the Yorkshire followers changed dramatically after

Wardle's journalist 'ghost' had brought shivers of disdain upon an affronted cricketer. Burnet acknowledges that his position as Yorkshire captain would have been untenable if the *Daily Mail* articles had not been written. Wardle would have gone to Australia as an England player and probably joined another county. Nottinghamshire were widely tipped to obtain his signature. They had made Johnny a handsome offer.

Wardle's bold and unashamed words had the effect of placing the seal of approval on Burnet's captaincy and discipline. Burnet shed his villain's cap for that of a hero on his first appearance at Headingley after the publication of the articles.

> From the moment I appeared out of the dressing-room I was cheered all the way out to the middle. I took guard and they were still standing and applauding me. Just bear in mind, I'd done nothing then. All I'd done was to *sack* Johnny Wardle. I had to wait for the cheers to subside before I faced my first ball. The opposing wicket-keeper turned to me and said: 'Well, you've got your answer there, skipper.'

The former Yorkshire captain says Wardle's departure brought an immediate gain in team harmony. In the following season, the year of Yorkshire's championship triumph, even opponents were saying: 'What a pleasure it is to play against Yorkshire again. It is like a different team.'

Ronnie Burnet remains unrepentant about his part in the downfall of a cricketing giant.

> I had the highest possible regard for Johnny as a cricketer. What happened was an absolute tragedy. He should have been in the side for another 10 years. I would have loved to have captained him when he was a younger cricketer. He would not have become a sour man. But in 1958 his character and the way he approached the game, as far as Yorkshire were concerned, were luxuries we couldn't afford.

In 1984, less than a year before his death, Wardle was the principal guest at the annual dinner of the Baildon Cricket Club, Burnet's home club. Their feud had long been forgotten. Wardle brought lustre to the occasion, an evening of remarkable cricket talk. He spoke ruefully of ambitions unfulfilled because of his early departure from first-class cricket.

Johnny looked up from his notes and smiled at Burnet. 'I'm not getting at Ron,' he said. 'He's all right, is t'lad.' Burnet cherishes those forgiving words. Johnny did not hold any grudges. 'It sealed our reconciliation.'

# 10
# A Friendly Cage for a Lion

*'Johnny took the Lancashire League utterly seriously. He paid us all an enormous compliment.' – Rishton C. C. captain.*

THE radio announcement of Johnny Wardle's dismissal by Yorkshire in July 1958 produced a swift response in Lancashire. The six o'clock report signalled a hasty conference in Nelson. Less than two hours later a four-man delegation arrived at Wardle's home in Wakefield. Johnny was cutting his lawn when the Nelson officials produced their credentials. He told them: 'My, that was bloody quick.' A four-figure deal was agreed in 45 minutes.

Nelson offered Wardle £1,100 to join them as professional in 1959, an indication of his worth as a cricket personality and drawing card. The fee was the highest paid by Nelson since Ray Lindwall, the Australian fast bowler, had been their professional in 1952. Johnny, never a mercenary in financial matters, later suffered qualms of conscience at accepting this astronomical fee. As one member of the family relates, he pondered deeply on the size of the remuneration. He had some sleepless nights. During his second season at Nelson he consulted with his employers. 'You are paying me too much,' he said. His proposal was unusual but entirely in keeping with his character. The salary was reduced by £200 to the relief of both Johnny and a thankful club.

This instance of Wardle's integrity is remembered by Ken Hartley, the former Nelson chairman and a long-standing committee man. The problem of having a man condemned as a Yorkshire dissident in their ranks was overcome by Wardle's exemplary conduct at Nelson and in his later association with Rishton. Hartley says: 'Johnny was quick to praise his colleagues; he just wanted the ball; and we never had any trouble with him.'

Neville Wood was the Nelson captain in Wardle's first season with the Lancashire League club. Wood, fearful of Johnny's fiery reputation in county cricket, took the precaution of travelling to Scarborough to meet Ronnie Burnet, the Yorkshire captain. Burnet told him that he would have to assert his authority. 'You have got to be boss,' was the instruction. It was countermanded by Wardle at a later meeting with the Nelson captain. Johnny said: 'We'll get on all right as long as tha' does as tha's told.'

Wardle, like his Yorkshire predecessor, Hedley Verity, discovered an appreciation of his gifts in Lancashire. Thirty years before, Verity had gone to Lancashire as an apprentice to sharpen his skills as a bowler. Wardle's journey across the Pennines came in his maturity as a troubled and outraged cricketer. It was to prove a therapeutic time for him, even though his considerable talents ought to have remained at the service of first-class cricket. His lights shone bright and warm in a friendly camp. But throughout his reign in Lancashire League cricket his admiring hosts at Nelson and Rishton were made aware that these were wasted years. Other sterner challenges were denied him.

Johnny Wardle was one of the last great international cricketers to delight the knowledgeable supporters of clubs striving for honours within a 30-mile section of Lancashire. On this small, illustrious stage he followed in the rampaging footsteps of Nelson's great West Indian, Learie Constantine, the pioneering professional of the 1930s, and hard on the heels of a galaxy of post-war entertainers. Among these were Everton Weekes, who hit 195, the highest score in a league match, for Bacup against Enfield in 1949; the late Collie Smith, another fine West Indian cricketer, who scored a magnificent 306 not out for Burnley in the Worsley Cup match against Lowerhouse in 1959; and Australian Bill Alley, who hit over 1,000 runs in five successive seasons at Colne. The highest number of runs scored in one season in the Lancashire League is credited to Everton Weekes. In 1951 at Bacup, Weekes had the astonishing aggregate of 1,518 runs. His nearest competitor was Bobby Simpson, the Australian captain, who scored 1,444 runs for Accrington in 1959.

Wardle's swagger was more constrained than that of other glamorous cricketers; but, in the view of one associate of those years, his impact on the league was more telling and significant.

> The Lancashire League fitted him like a glove. It meant something to him. He hadn't just drifted in from Port of Spain to hit six spectacular fifties and then drift out again. With Johnny you had the authentic whiff of English professionalism. You felt that every word he said carried the stamp of experience.

The approval came not just from Wardle's fellow players and spectators. The league committees and officials also warmed to him and were won over by his dedication. At Blackburn, one of the major league headquarters, they could not do enough for this likeable and earnest man. 'They were proud of caging or containing a lion,' recalls a former team-mate. There was a sense of wonderment that they had captured the heart and mind of such a rebellious spirit. 'He seems to be happy with us,' said the administrators in a tone of quiet rejoicing as if anxious not to break the spell.

Wardle made his first appearances in the Lancashire League in the late summer of 1958 as deputy professional at Rishton. He replaced Alfred Valentine, the West Indian left-arm bowler, who had to return home because of his mother's illness. Wardle's debut for Rishton against local rivals, East Lancashire, attracted a crowd of 3,000. They were accompanied by a covey of national newspaper correspondents drawn like locusts to feast on the anger of a controversial man. There was heavy rain on the morning of the match but it did not deter Jack Marsden, the Rishton president, and his army of helpers on this important day. From his home near the Blackburn Road ground Marsden emerged with a pair of new blankets which were still wrapped in their cellophane packing. These were used to soak up the water and wrung through many times by an old mangle which had served the club so well in other downpours over the years.

In canny Lancashire fashion, Rishton had also taken the precaution of insuring the game. The match was spared but the necessary amount of rain had fallen in the specified time. As a reward for their prudence the club received £100 to add to the gate receipts of £200. Johnny Wardle had only a modest success, taking 2 wickets and scoring 15 runs; but as they banked their cash Rishton assured their Yorkshire guest of a warm welcome if he chose to join the club on a permanent basis.

Nelson's agreement with Wardle meant that the reunion had to be postponed for four more years. In his first season at Nelson Johnny paraded his skills in inimitably deft style. He took 101 league wickets and hoisted the Seedhill club to a runners-up place. It was the beginning of a phase of ardent professionalism which was to yield him 1,143 wickets in ten years in the Lancashire League. Only four other players – Fred Duerr (Bacup and Ramsbottom); Billy Cook (Enfield, Burnley, Lowerhouse and Colne); Tom Lancaster (Colne); and Alf Pollard (Colne and Nelson) – had taken more wickets in the league. Duerr's total of over 2,000 wickets was spread over 28 seasons; Pollard spent 19 seasons in taking 1,390 wickets; and the achievements of Cook and Lancaster were also gained over longer periods.

Wardle's professional rivals in his era were celebrities of world-class stature. From South Africa came the rugged campaigner, Eddie Barlow; the West Indian representatives were Basil Butcher, Seymour Nurse, Wes Hall and the fiercely antagonistic Charlie Griffith and Roy Gilchrist; and the Australian opposition included Bobby Simpson, Neil Hawke and Bob Cowper. There was also a renewal of his jousts with Tony Lock. Lock found the lure of League cricket lucrative enough to return from Australia to take over as professional at Ramsbottom before moving back into county cricket with Leicestershire.

John Kay, a shrewd observer of Lancashire cricket, remembers how both Wardle and Lock upheld their highest standards in Lancashire. They were appalled at the slovenly fielding in the league and exerted their authority to bring about improvements.

> Temperamentally each was ideally suited to the league demands. They were allowed full play of their talents. Long spells of bowling, an opportunity to bat far higher than was their custom in the first-class sphere, and a major say in field placings and tactics generally brought both Lock and Wardle to the forefront match after match and week after week. Each knew failure but success was generally within their reach and it is of no little significance that each knew and went out of his way to impress upon his amateur colleagues the value of good fielding.

The relationship between Lock and Wardle was just as wary in the Lancashire League as in first-class cricket. In one match in the 1960s Lock dismissed Rishton for 72. During the tea interval he was complimented by Tommy Welsh, the Rishton chairman, on his fine bowling. 'Yes, I did well,' replied Tony. 'But this bugger [pointing to Johnny] will bowl us out for even less.' Lock's prophecy was fulfilled in another dazzling conquest.

Johnny and Tony were resolute bowling partners for a League eleven against Lancashire in 1965. Lock took 7 for 39 to dismiss the county for 162 in their first innings. The Yorkshire-Surrey pair were at their artful best in restricting Lancashire to 117 for 6 in the second innings. Their opponents were kept on a tight rein. Lancashire were never allowed to slip into a canter as they failed in the challenge of scoring 208 in less than three hours.

At Nelson Alan Haigh was the wicket-keeper during Wardle's four seasons at the Seedhill club. He recalls:

Ninety-five per cent of the opposing batsmen couldn't pick him. The ball came off the wicket very quickly. He flighted his googly so well. He could be very funny at times. He once said to me: 'You look like a 'keeper because you can't bat.'

Haigh adds: 'What I liked about Johnny was that he always wanted to do well. He was depressed on his rare, unsuccessful days.'

Wardle secured 343 wickets at an average of 11.94 runs each at Nelson. In 1959, when Nelson were runners-up in the League championship, he was a member of the League side which defeated a strong Lancashire eleven by 71 runs at Old Trafford. Collie Smith, the West Indian batsman and Burnley professional, who was later to be killed in a road accident, scored 71 out of the League XI's first innings total of 274. Wardle's contribution was 51 in 25 minutes, including 22 in one over. Smith hit a century in the second innings and Lancashire were set a target of 206 for victory. They were bowled out for 135, Wardle obtaining 4 wickets for 33 runs in 21 overs. Johnny also took two catches off Smith, who returned figures of 4 wickets for 40 runs.

In 1960, against Lowerhouse, Nelson were dismissed for 73 but still won by 17 runs as Wardle took 6 wickets for 11 runs. In the following season in which Nelson again had to be content with a League runners-up place, there was an even more dramatic change in fortunes. Nelson could only manage 51 against the searing pace of West Indian fast bowler, Chester Watson, who took 6 wickets for 5 runs for Church. Wardle produced a staggering riposte. His figures were 5 wickets for 16 runs and Church were bowled out for 50!

Wardle's all-round talents also produced more than 5,000 runs in Lancashire League cricket. In April, 1960 he was unbeaten on 94 in a third-wicket partnership of 121 with his captain Neville Wood against Rawtenstall. Later in the same season there was another three-figure stand for the third wicket – 120 against Lowerhouse – and Johnny's share was a typically buccaneering 67. In his last season at Nelson, in 1962, Wardle hit his only century for the club at home to Todmorden. It helped to establish a new third-wicket record partnership of 174 for Nelson. Wardle scored 124, including 4 sixes and 18 fours, in 91 minutes. Denis Smith, with 76 not out, was his partner in the run spree. Nelson totalled 224 for 3 declared and Todmorden were bowled out for 143. Wardle followed his big hitting by taking 6 wickets for 39 runs. Rain intervened to prevent Wardle and Nelson from confirming their supremacy over Todmorden in the Worsley Cup final in 1962. The game could not be completed and Nelson and Todmorden each held the trophy for six months – the only occasion on which this has occurred.

Wardle is remembered by Nelson as one of their finest acquisitions, a signal tribute from a club boasting a glittering roll-call of professionals – from Australia's Ted McDonald and West Indian Learie Constantine in the 1920s and 1930s to Lala Amarnath (India) and Ray Lindwall (Australia) in later years. He impressed everyone at the Seedhill Club with his professional approach to the game and his still dominant skills. Ken Hartley recalls: 'Johnny was a character and his sense of humour had carried him through many bad times.'

In lighter moments Johnny was always able to reduce crowds to side-splitting laughter with his antics, which included taking off the umpire's hat as he came in to bowl. At Burnley he once took a wicket with a rag on the ball. The humour bubbled over in his business dealings, too. Johnny used to sell cricket boot laces at 1s 6d a pair in the Rishton dressing-room. They became so popular that he increased the price by a shilling. On another occasion he received a request for a short-handled bat. The following week the buyer unwrapped the parcel containing the bat and complained that the handle was too long. Johnny said that the correctly sized handle would be available for the next match. The Rishton player stared at the bat in disbelief when it was handed to him. Johnny had, indeed, shortened the handle by one and a half inches. His method had been to saw through the rubber grip. 'You've sawn the handle,' said the incredulous batsman. Johnny replied: 'I'm building a 50ft shed at home. If I can't make a short-handled bat, it is time I packed up.'

One of the best stories, although deliciously funny in retrospect, was in a serious vein. It was another example of Wardle's crusade against bowlers with illegal actions. Wardle was then involved in a feud with West Indian fast bowler, Roy Gilchrist, a wild man in many accounts. Johnny was convinced that Gilchrist was a 'chucker' (he later made the same charge against another West Indian, Charlie Griffith) and had voiced his complaint in an article in a local newspaper.

In order to confirm his view Wardle put up a camera outside the Bacup pavilion to film Gilchrist in action. The Bacup club officials insisted that the camera should be taken down; Gilchrist stopped bowling and refused to continue until the filming ceased. The game came to an abrupt halt. We can be sure that anger was the prevailing mood in the home camp. Hilarity probably ruled in the Nelson dressing-room, with players gagging their chuckles in handkerchiefs, when Johnny brought his camera inside to proceed more secretly with his investigation. The film, as far as can be ascertained, no longer exists. It would make instructive viewing.

David Lomas, then an aspiring 17-year-old and later to become one of Wardle's keenest fielding allies, recalls the Yorkshire bowler's arrival at the village club of Rishton in 1963. Johnny took nine wickets in his first game at Ramsbottom. 'We had a team coach, a Corporation bus, actually,' remembers Lomas. 'It would drop us down in Rishton. We'd then call in at the local pub for a pint before going home.' As he walked up the hill, he passed little groups of welcoming, curious villagers. They all wanted to know how their new professional had fared at Ramsbottom. Lomas relayed the news of Wardle's success. 'Nine wickets, eh,' went up the chorus. 'It looks as if we've got a good 'un.' Rishton had, indeed, made a great capture. Wardle was the only professional to take 100 wickets in the season. He repeated the feat on three other occasions; and altogether he secured 705 league and cup wickets in six seasons.

Rishton, in 1987 the professional home of perhaps the finest of modern batsmen, Vivian Richards, has ties with other legendary cricketers. It welcomed, in 1895, a player who is regarded as the greatest bowler in the history of the game, the mercurial S. F. Barnes. It was his first professional engagement. Barnes was followed in the course of time by an illustrious line of professionals. They included Bert Vogler, the South African leg-break bowler, one of the redoubtable 'googly quartet' which toured England in 1907; Jack Newstead, a key member of Lord Hawke's Yorkshire team; Bill Merritt, the New Zealand leg-spinner of the 1930s; and the supremely gifted Subhash Gupte, the first of the world-class Indian spinners to emerge after the Second World War.

The mill-owners of Rishton were the benefactors, often guaranteeing bank overdrafts in hard times, in the Lancashire village. They enabled the club to flourish in the shadow of its powerful neighbour, East Lancashire, at Blackburn. The streets of Rishton, each belonging to various mills, were built on a rectangular basis and housed the weavers of the community. The weavers who played cricket for Rishton were always sure of a job. One former president, Jack Marsden, described by one Rishton man as the 'last of the Pharaohs', was one of the mill-owners who brought prosperity in work and sport to the village in the 1930s.

The mingling of renowned professionals from all over the world and lowly amateurs was an interesting phenomenon. The criterion in the Lancashire League was that only the best professionals were good enough to grace club ranks. 'There was a big discrepancy between the glamour of the professional and the lads who were playing with him,' comments former Rishton captain, Bernard Hurst. 'The imbalance was less when Wardle arrived because people were becoming more affluent.' Hurst, like many observers, believes that Johnny Wardle left first-class cricket before he should have done.

> He came into a league situation, which he could easily have dismissed as a frolic, and said to himself: 'This is where I am and this is where I am going to be the best. This is where I am going to make my living.'

The former Rishton captain remembers his old colleague as like a 'man hewn out of rock'.

> He could be utterly crushing and frighten people to death. His own standards were so very high. Johnny approved of skill in others but he was ruthless with those players who failed to measure up. To be taken seriously by him was quite a compliment. He operated on the basis that for Rishton to do well he had to do well. This suited him perfectly.

Wardle, making his weekly journeys to Rishton from his home at Thorne — a two-and-a-half-hour drive in his powerful sports car — was always among the first to arrive for matches. 'Everything was in time,' says Bernard Hurst. 'There was none of this last-minute unreliability. He took the league utterly seriously and paid us all an enormous compliment.' In the period of quiet contemplation before the start of play, Johnny would park his car beside the scoreboard, eat his lunch sandwiches, and then examine the wicket. The Rishton captain would then be told whether to bat or field. 'You know what to do today,' Johnny would say. 'Put them in.'

Wardle was meticulous in his attention to wickets. The Rishton groundsman of his time was a man called Bill Shakespeare, a former First World War army captain. He had, it seems, been a dandy in the 1930s, an extravagant character in the Lord Peter Wimsey mould, given to wearing smart check suits, linen shirts and a bow tie. 'By the time we knew Bill he was in decline,' says Hurst. Shakespeare forged a bond with Wardle and the two men spent hours discussing the preparation of wickets at Rishton. The one-time dilettante elected to occupy his final years looking after the village cricket field. Shakespeare exchanged his smart clothes for dungarees and a little jockey cap. He became progressively dirtier in his new job. Wardle, intent on producing wickets which were crucial to him as a bowler, would say: 'Get that grass off, Bill. Give it another cut. There is too much on.'

Johnny insisted on the Rishton wickets being given regular applications of marl. The treatment was intended to reduce the pace in the wickets so that they ended up with the texture of Blackpool sands. It did, to their undisguised disgust, nullify the speed of West Indian bowlers such as Wes Hall. The brown, shorn wicket in the green field was an oasis of delight for Wardle; but it produced bitter complaints from opponents. Neil Hawke, the Australian fast bowler and Nelson professional, once said: 'I have learned my trade as a cricketer but he is defeating my skills with his marled wicket.' For Wardle, particularly when rain intervened, cricket was blissful at Rishton. 'The least drop of rain on the wicket made it bite for his spin,' says Bernard Hurst. 'It would turn and lift and Johnny was virtually unplayable in such conditions.'

With Rishton, Wardle would usually bowl 'seam up' with the new ball before turning to his orthodox slow deliveries. Only occasionally did he revert to the chinaman and googlies. David Lomas recalls one piece of advice offered by Wardle. He told the Rishton amateurs: 'You never beat good batsmen off the wicket. You always beat them in the air.'

Wardle was not affected, as in his county days, by the problem of obtaining the right end for his bowling skills. His choice was not disputed at Rishton. In one match he erred in his judgement and conceded about 40 runs before changing to the other end. He then proceeded to take 6 wickets for 12 runs. 'Bloody hell, John, you bowled well today,' remarked one Rishton player. Wardle, remembering his earlier lack of success, replied: 'I slipped up. I picked the wrong end. I could see when I was bowling where the grass was lying.'

There was immense respect for the scale of Johnny's cricket knowledge at Rishton and elsewhere in Lancashire. One East Lancashire leg-spinner remembers Wardle's encouragement. 'I bowled to Johnny in one match and he gave me a bit of tap, carting me out of the ground two or three times. He wasn't quite so certain when I bowled a quicker one at him.'

In the club bar afterwards Wardle told his opponent that he ought to bowl this ball a little more often. 'You listen to the good ones – and they didn't come much better than Wardle,' says the Lancastrian. In the following match East Lancashire were again opposed to Rishton in a cup match. 'Johnny hit me for a couple of boundaries, so I thought I'd try a flat, faster ball. It nipped in pretty quickly and he was caught. Johnny gave me a knowing look and laughed.' One East Lancashire committee man could hardly contain his glee after the match. 'He got you there,' he told Wardle. Johnny replied: 'I don't know, I keep telling these lads what to do. And their average goes up and my average goes down.'

Bernard Hurst recalls how Wardle brought a new dimension to the concept of field placings at Rishton. 'You became perfectly aware that a yard either way was crucial to his strategy.' Wardle could be brutal in his criticism when important catches were dropped and runs unnecessarily conceded in the field. One young amateur to suffer was David Smith, the son of former Middlesex player, Jim Smith. In his first match for Rishton Smith dropped four catches off Wardle in the Yorkshireman's opening overs. After watching the unfortunate lad spill three chances in the same position in the outfield, Johnny moved him to another place, apparently less hazardous, on the boundary. The boy seemed safe and secure but the ball, as if drawn by a magnet, soared in his direction again. He dropped the catch. An angry Johnny called out to the Rishton captain: 'Go and tell that lad to just walk about because he is no ....... use on a cricket field.'

David Lomas and Mick Eddleston were two close fielding allies who earned Wardle's trust at Rishton. Lomas fielded in the gully and Eddleston at very short leg. Bernard Hurst recalls:

> Johnny depended on inspiring these two young lads to be brave. And they were brave. It was quite reckless to stand there, match after match, without helmets or any other form of protection. But you could rely on Johnny dropping the ball accurately on the spot.

Lomas also remembers his afternoon vigils, perched perilously close to the edge of the bat. 'John told us that if he won the Lancashire League bowling prize we would get fifty pence a catch. We never got nowt.'

Wardle was, as befits a Yorkshireman, careful in financial matters. After his hard upbringing, he knew the value of money but he was never greedy. 'Johnny did not want anything that he hadn't taken his shirt off to earn. What he got he fought for,' says one close friend. Jim Clarke, the Lancashire League secretary, believes that Wardle received around £700 a season at Rishton. The honourable, considerate cricketer was prepared to accept his pay in instalments, a great boon for the village club constantly struggling to balance the books. Wardle's attitude was: 'If I want something I will ask for it.' Half his money was paid at the end of July and the rest in the following March.

In the 1962 season the Matthew Brown Brewery, the Lancashire League's present sponsors, had introduced £50 awards for amateur and professional aggregate batting and bowling performances. As the leading professional bowler, with 121 wickets, Wardle first received the award in 1963 and was to win the Matthew Brown trophy three times in four seasons. Ironically, in 1964, when his 122 wickets represented his best season in the league, Charlie Griffith's tally of 144 wickets deprived him of the trophy.

Ken Grieves, the Australian who played for Lancashire with distinction, was another batting recipient of the award during his time as professional at Accrington. He cherishes his memories of Wardle as a great bowler and gentleman. Grieves, a brilliant fieldsman, remembers one league duel with Johnny.

> I remember taking a catch, left-handed and at full-stretch, at mid-wicket off a full-blooded hit by Johnny. I will leave it to you to imagine what he said and also what I said to myself when I was given out lbw to a ball from a Rishton amateur that I allowed to hit the top of my thigh.

In the return game at Rishton Wardle bowled Grieves 'neck and crop' with a good length ball that pitched outside his off-stump and came back to hit his leg-stump. 'Johnny', says Grieves, 'was bowling round the wicket and delivering the ball with orthodox left-hand spin.' It was an unlikely dispatch and both Wardle and Grieves, discussing the dismissal over a pint, agreed that the ball must have deviated after hitting a hole in the pitch.

Rishton won the Worsley Cup twice (in 1964 and 1967) and were league runners-up three times in succession during Wardle's reign at Blackburn Road. These were exciting times for the village club and the events of 1964 took pride of place. As a prelude to the glories of the season, there was a spectacular display of hitting by Wardle against Ramsbottom. He made a sedate start to his innings with eight singles in 18 minutes. He then hit 45 runs in two successive eight-ball overs. Twenty-seven runs, including six fours, were taken off one over and there were two more boundaries in the next over. Wardle capped his batting accomplishment by taking 7 wickets for 46 runs to ensure a comfortable win for Rishton.

Bernard Hurst considers that the culmination of Wardle's time at Rishton, in terms of playing achievement and in his rivalry with other professionals, was the Worsley Cup final against Burnley in 1964. This was the season dominated by West Indian fast bowler, Charlie Griffith, then making his debut with Burnley. Griffith, at the height of his terrifying powers and later to trouble England sorely, established a league record of 144 wickets. Burnley won the championship with 70 points. Rishton challenged them strongly throughout the summer and gained the runners-up place by beating Accrington on the last ball of the game in the penultimate match of the season. Hurst still shudders at the memory of Griffith's pace.

It was not merely a question of speed that was in a different dimension to the average club player's definition of fast bowling. It was also a peculiar and questionable delivery where the arm emerged suddenly and late from behind his head in what many good judges (including Wardle) thought at the time was a throw. Griffith's attitude did not immediately invite the term chivalrous and many club batsmen were dismissed by a full-pitched ball or a yorker after the preceding short one had unsettled them.

The problem had been starkly demonstrated at Turf Moor in a league match. Rishton, with a succession of victories behind them, were physically smashed to defeat by the ferocity of Griffith's bowling. 'We were annihilated on a fairly inadequate pitch. The ball was lifting from just short of a length and Griffith was not making any concessions,' says Hurst. These were the days before helmets and sophisticated protective aids. Several players were hurt. Wardle told his team-mates that England would not have made 100 in such hostile conditions. It was in this match that Johnny, never one for heroics as a batsman, amusingly declined the challenge. 'You're in, John,' said the Rishton amateurs. Wardle had just lit a cigarette. 'Don't put that bloody cigarette out,' he said, 'I'll be back in a minute.' Jack Chew salvaged Rishton's honour at the cost of loss of work through injury. He scored an unbeaten half-century as Rishton subsided to 97 all out.

Chew was a professional footballer who had played for Burnley in a Wembley Cup Final. He was also, as his defiance against Griffith demonstrated, a very fine batsman, a county cricketer in all but name. Chew was immensely respected by Wardle. 'This was one of the keys to Johnny's time with us,' says another Rishton cricketer. 'Jack, like Johnny, was a working-class lad, who had earned his living as a professional sportsman.' Their accord as players and mature men was an important element of harmony in the team.

Jack Chew, against the odds, repeated his league feat in the Worsley Cup final against Burnley. It was a superb contest watched by a crowd of over 7,000 and producing record gate receipts of over £700. Wardle took 7 wickets for 83 runs as Burnley lost their last 9 wickets for 96 runs. On the previous day in the league against Haslingden there had been a disconcerting number of dropped catches. At Turf Moor the infection was checked, all the chances were accepted, and Burnley were restricted to 142.

Griffith, though, was there to renew his combat with opponents he had demoralised a few weeks earlier. Bernard Hurst recalls:

> It was a better wicket for the final than the one in use in the league match. But there was still the smell of the Colosseum about the place.

We were poor mortals being thrown to a very big lion. Our dressing-room must have resembled the Somme before the First World War push. Jack Chew achieved that season what to me is still the finest cricket achievement of my lifetime against one of the most feared bowlers of modern times, armed with only a floppy green cap (an Australian gift) and his trusted Gunn and Moore bat. Jack was an inspiring giant-killer and I will never cease to marvel at the technique and courage that fired his defence, spiced as it was by simple Blackburn bloodymindedness. You might get him out but you would never get him to retreat.

Rishton lost their first wicket without a run on the board and faced an uphill task in averaging almost four runs an over. They also had to accept the unpalatable fact that Griffith would almost certainly bowl throughout their innings. The second wicket fell at 51 and the third at 57. Chew was joined by Kevin Flatley in what proved to be a match-winning fourth wicket partnership. 'Both players moved behind the line of the ball and gradually, to our relief and astonishment, we realised we were winning the battle,' says Hurst. Burnley's signal of surrender was confirmed when Griffith, suffering a real or imagined leg injury, went on to a short run. 'The balance had swung so far our way that we became unstoppable.' Chew scored his second unbeaten 50 of the season against Burnley. Flatley hit 44 and Rishton won in stirring style by seven wickets.

Three years later the Worsley Cup was raised again at Rishton. Their opponents were Accrington, who had lost only one league game during the season. Accrington were dismissed for 102, Wardle taking 5 wickets for 56 runs. Chew played another worthy innings of 33 but Rishton were uncomfortably placed at 60 for 5. It was left to Wardle and Jim Smith to ease the anxieties and lead their team to victory by 5 wickets.

Wardle's skills as a bowler did not flag as he moved into his forties. But the claims of his thriving social club at Thorne began to take priority and the strain of travelling hundreds of miles to matches in Lancashire also took their toll of even his resilient physique. Jim Clarke considered that Wardle was as good a bowler when he retired, at the age of 45, as he was when he first entered the League 10 years earlier.

Wardle maintained his exacting standards until the end. Stunning bowling returns of 7, 8 and 9 wickets were common-place. Against Ramsbottom he secured 9 wickets for 38 runs, the first 5 for 2 runs in only 18 deliveries. He twice took two wickets with successive balls. 'If we scored 150 with Johnny, we were sure to win. And even if we only put up 100, we were in with a chance,' says one Rishton associate.

The tactical blueprint, within the constraints of five hours' playing time, was not as simple as that statement suggests. It was much more refined in practice. Rishton, in fact, invariably batted first. The art was to set their opponents a realistic target so that they would go for the runs against Wardle. 'You wouldn't want them to shut up the game,' says Bernard Hurst. 'We had to make it tempting even against batsmen of the quality of Seymour Nurse, Eddie Barlow and Basil Butcher.'

Johnny Wardle's distinguished reign in the Lancashire League coincided with another successful period as professional with Cambridgeshire in the Minor Counties championship. He was persuaded to take up this appointment by Maurice Crouch, the enthusiastic Cambridgeshire captain. It was an influential signing and marked a turning point in the county's fortunes. In 1963 – Wardle's opening season – Cambridgeshire won the Minor Counties title for the first time in their history. Johnny took 81 wickets in 9 matches, a remarkable performance; and in 7 seasons his tally was 316 wickets at an average of 14.40 runs each. Crouch remembers:

> We certainly had a very good side, but I very much doubt if we would have finished top but for Johnny. He completely mesmerised most of the opposition, mainly with his 'back-of-the-hand' stuff.
>
> When the news got into the press that Johnny had signed for us, one or two first-class players that I knew, warned me that he was difficult to handle. If that were true, I didn't find it so. I always had the best of relations with him: I liked him and I learned a lot from him during the season. I certainly had to calm things down on one or two occasions when he was taunted by certain players in the opposition. However, usually they had deliberately set out to ruffle him and knew he was liable to bite.

Before the 1963 season started Wardle played for Cambridgeshire in a one-day friendly match against Nottinghamshire. He bowled well but several dropped catches limited his return to three wickets. 'Johnny had a dry sense of humour and one of our younger players, Derek Wing, had cause to wonder what sort of cricketer we had signed on,' Crouch recalls.

Wing failed to hold on to 'skier' at deep mid-on off Wardle's bowling. Johnny told the fielding miscreant: 'Did that ball hit you on the head, lad?' The Cambridgeshire youngster assured Wardle that he had escaped unscathed. The new professional looked at him in anguish and said: 'Well, it bloody well should have done.' Crouch insists that this was a good-humoured refrain. 'The more we played with him, the more we appreciated his witticisms. When I pinned up the batting order on the dressing-room door, with Johnny at No. 9, he casually said to me: "Cambs must be a good batting side, skipper: I used to bat higher than that for England." ' Crouch thinks his evaluation of Wardle was correct. 'When Johnny went in they immediately put on their fast bowler. He didn't trouble the scorer on that occasion.'

One South Yorkshireman, David Farnell, exiled in Cambridgeshire, remembers being paired as a leg-spinner bowler with his boyhood idol in a match, his first for the county, against Nottinghamshire's second eleven at Collingham, Newark, in 1964. 'I was at the ground early and made my way to speak to Wardle. I felt as though I knew him though it was several years since I had seen him in action at Bramall Lane. I approached him, gave him my name, and said I used to watch him playing for Yorkshire at Sheffield.' Wardle closely examined his new team-mate. 'Are tha' playing for us, then?' he asked. 'Yes', was the proud response. 'Well', said Johnny, 'tha'd best button up thi' flies, lad.'

At tea on the final day of the match Nottinghamshire were poised for victory. The names on the scorecard – Smedley, Poole, Gillhouley and Stead, all emerging or seasoned professionals – demonstrates why they were favourites to win. The subsequent events revived the images of his boyhood for Farnell. The vital difference was that he was also in the spotlight along with the irrepressible Johnny. 'Wardle took one end and the captain gave me the other end and things started to happen,' recalls Farnell. 'Good players prodded forward to Wardle clearly without any idea as to where the ball was going.' Seven catches were taken at short-leg. Every ball was bang on the spot. Nottinghamshire collapsed to 111 all out. Wardle took 6 wickets and Farnell 3. When Farnell returned home that evening his wife was in the garden talking to neighbours. He went up to her, holding out his arm, and said: 'Pinch me! Make sure it's not a dream. I've just been bowling with Johnny Wardle and we've bowled out Notts seconds.'

Farnell's other principal memories of this Cambridgeshire cricket association are of fielding at slip or short leg to the Yorkshire and England bowler. He remembers the 'jaunty little run in, knees high, the left arm round the back and the arch of the back' and how Wardle would say: 'tha' gets it all from the back, tha' knows'. One day he asked Johnny for his advice on identifying the spin. 'Watch t'batsman's feet,' said Wardle. 'If he goes forward, stay put; if he goes back, run like bloody 'ell.' Farnell does not recall feeling in any danger as he stood a yard and a half off the bat behind square to Wardle.

The emphasis on field placings is another strong impression. Just a wave here and a flap of the hand there. You had to keep watching and concentrating. Johnny bowled to plans. He meant the batsman to do something specific with every ball. And if time mattered he would slow the game without it showing. 'Chuck the ball back to me so I have to pause,' he used to say.

One story, possibly apocryphal, was related time and time again in the Minor Counties pavilions. A particular player was enjoying unusual success against Wardle, driving the ball straight and on either side of the wicket. Accompanying each handsome stroke was his audible cry: 'I read it, I read it.' Johnny rubbed his chin in puzzlement and approached the batsman in the bar afterwards. 'Look here,' he said, 'I've bowled at the world's greatest batsmen and not one of them claims to read me like you did today. How did you do it?' 'Dead easy,' said the batting adventurer. 'I come out. I swing the bat. If the ball goes to mid-on it was the chinaman, if it goes to mid-off it was the googly.'

A last recollection of Wardle in his Minor Counties days is of a more respectful contest. It concerns the meeting of Johnny with his old England colleague and Middlesex rival, Bill Edrich. Wardle and Edrich were opponents in a match between Cambridgeshire and Norfolk. Their rivalry was as intense as ever. Norfolk wanted around 70 to win and narrowly succeeded in their quest by three wickets. Edrich scored 40 of the runs and Wardle took 6 wickets. Not a word was exchanged in the middle but there were expressions of praise as they walked off together. 'Well batted, Bill,' said Johnny. 'Well bowled, Johnny,' said Bill. It was a reflection of the esteem which existed between two wise old campaigners.

The wheel turned full circle when Johnny Wardle returned to South Yorkshire cricket pastures to end his career on a triumphant note. The setting for his last bowling endeavours was Barnby Dun, a little Doncaster League club. It was a gesture of thanks by Johnny to the club members who had supported his cricket school and country club at nearby Thorne. Wardle headed the league bowling averages in two seasons with Barnby Dun. In 1969 he took 107 wickets in 18 matches at an average of 5.34 runs each. He was the first bowler to take 100 wickets in the history of the League. Only one other bowler, Tommy Wass, a former Nottinghamshire player, had approached the feat with 91 wickets for Bullcroft Main in 1923.

Wardle's century of wickets included six in Barnby Dun's victory by four wickets over Warmsworth in the Doncaster and District League First Division final in September 1969. The victory marked yet another milestone for Barnby Dun; it was the first time they had won the title. In 1970 Wardle secured 93 wickets at an average of 6.46 runs each. His match returns on sporting wickets indicated hysteria or desperation on the part of opposing batsmen; only eight clubs reached three figures and totals ranged from 20 to 60, 80 or 90 on Johnny's more indulgent days. He was aided in his successes by a talented local wicket-keeper, Frankish, who made over 30 stumpings off his bowling in two seasons.

Wardle, even in these humble surroundings, did not depart from his stern professionalism; he was always punctual as a player and stringent in his wicket inspections. He was an invigorating taskmaster on the field and was known to observe 'you can hide one player, but you can't hide nine'. As a bowler he opened with the new ball and then switched to spinners. There was the usual eye to the right end. In his first season with Barnby Dun he bowled unchanged; but he later relented at the insistence not of the opposition but of his own team. His response to umpires who asked him if he wanted his sweater was to say: 'Not until September.'

Johnny was puzzled at times by the ways of village cricket. He was inclined to get cross when the groundsman, in the interests of retaining grass on the square, brought the sprinkler into regular use in dry weather. 'You have the best bloody slow bowler in England playing for you,' he would say. 'I don't want to see that hosepipe any more. However do you think I am going to get any bounce?'

Johnny was still squaring his broad shoulders, jealously guarding his bowling average, as he championed Barnby Dun. After he had taken 100 wickets for the club, he said: 'You lads dropped so many catches that I had to get everyone out twice.'

# 11
# The Happy Cricketer

*'When you are as good as Johnny you can act the goat a bit'* – Geoff Cope.

'WA-ARDLE'S IN.' The eyes of thousands were riveted to the scene when Johnny, his shoulders squared and his cap set at a jaunty angle, strode in to bat. Everyone, boys and girls and adults alike, moved forward on their seats in expectation of another glorious feast of hitting.

If Wardle was in a tempestuous mood, wielding his bat with his immensely powerful forearms, run-making was a fast and furious affair. He was as unpredictable (and disconcerting to his opponents) as Ian Botham. We remember the gigantic sixes and the mis-hits which spiralled over quaking fieldsmen. On those occasions his innings had a careless rapture.

He was not just a six-hitting cavalier. Jim Swanton remembers him as a dangerous and often decisive batsman for Yorkshire and England. 'The virtue of Johnny's cricket did not end with his bowling at all.' Wardle's career figures of over 7,000 runs were achieved in critical as well as hilarious moments. Indeed, there were many good judges who felt he had the potential to become an all-rounder of merit.

In 1950 he demonstrated this potential with 733 runs and 174 wickets. But he is best remembered as a dasher at the crease. Against the MCC and Jim Laker at Lord's he crashed two sixes into the Grandstand and another into a neighbouring garden. In the pavilion there were murmurs of disapproval at such levity. One MCC member remarked: 'Agricultural, what?' A Yorkshireman in a nearby seat greeted the sally with disdain. 'Yes, but bloomin' fertile,' he quipped.

A. A. Thomson, in his book, *Cricket My Happiness*, tells the charming story of Wardle in another match at Lord's. A dull day's play was drifting drowsily to a close when Johnny emerged from the pavilion.

> At his first six-hit the crowd roared with delight; at his second they stood on the seats and cheered; at his third many of them were collapsing with half-joyous, half-hysterical laughter. We were told at school that Shakespeare always introduced a comedy scene to relieve the tension of his tragedy. If that was so, Johnny Wardle that evening played a scene equalling the combined efforts of Hamlet's gravediggers and the porter in Macbeth. By the force of his blows he might have awakened Duncan with his knocking.
>
> Smiling broadly, he made 22 off, I think, seven balls, and a few minutes later I found myself walking down St John's Wood Road along with 20,000 people, all laughing as if they had been witnessing the greatest joke in the world. But I imagine that Johnny, somewhere in the players' dressing-room, was laughing loudest of all.

Wardle's most spectacular batting feat was appropriately reserved for a Roses match. At Old Trafford, in 1951, Yorkshire had lost five wickets for 165 runs when Johnny embarked on a breathtaking assault on the Lancashire bowling. In 25 minutes before tea he cudgelled 36 runs, including five fours and two sixes. On the resumption he struck three more sixes off Tattersall to reach his 50 in 45 minutes. It was free, enterprising and uncomplicated cricket. There was one more six lofted high over mid-wicket in his innings of 79 – his highest in first-class cricket – in 70 minutes.

At Sheffield, in 1954, Brian Close joined Wardle on another batting rampage this time against Pakistan. His century in just over two hours hoisted the 300 to provide the ideal platform for Johnny. Jim Kilburn wrote:

> With co-operation from the fieldsmen Wardle entertained, and in the course of his conquest drove Pakistan to final demoralisation. They lost all idea of where to bowl and where to station themselves in the field, though on occasion they would have been helpless 30 yards outside it. Two of Wardle's three sixes to leg were as colossal, stupendous and gorgeously coloured as any film according to advertisement. His innings of 72 occupied 50 minutes. Adults cheered; children screamed. Bramall Lane sounded like a circus.

The smiles shone again at Bramall Lane against the South Africans in the following season. The issue was sealed in the tourists' favour when the seventh wicket fell at 97 in Yorkshire's second innings. Wardle created an innings approaching the fantastic by scoring 74 runs (out of 85) in 30 minutes, striking 6 sixes and 7 fours before he was bowled by Tayfield. He attacked the bowling with such vigour that in 17 minutes he had scored 50 runs – and had also been missed at slip. There were 2 sixes and 3 fours off Smith in the over of the squandered catch. Johnny hit 2 more sixes and 3 more fours in the 50, all magnificent blows and strokes of tremendous carry.

Wardle was often a man to dissolve a crisis for Yorkshire and England. At Hull in 1954, after his great bowling feat against Sussex, he recaptured the initiative for Yorkshire with batting of equal venom. In the middle of an innings of riotous stroke-play he was suddenly becalmed during an over from Robin Marlar, the Sussex off-spinner. Bowling over the wicket, Marlar pitched each ball outside the off-stump. To five of the balls Wardle lifted his bat high and allowed them to go through to the wicket-keeper. With exaggerated care, he leaned his bat against the stumps and walked over to the square-leg umpire. He then signalled to the perplexed Marlar to carry on bowling. The ground erupted with laughter and it was only after several minutes that play resumed. Marlar's last ball pitched on the same spot. Wardle again shouldered arms as if to say: 'Let's get on with the game.'

Ian Peebles said of Wardle that he had the gift of comic timing which put him in a class of his own. 'Perhaps the sincerest tribute I can pay him is to say that having seen the whole repertoire over the years it never grates and always makes me laugh.'

Godfrey Evans, Bob Appleyard and Trevor Bailey all remember Johnny as the jester on the field who never overplayed his act. Bailey remembers his old England colleague as a 'brilliant comic but not a funny man'. 'You did not walk into the dressing-room and fall about with laughter at his sallies, he was far too serious a man for that.' It is a view endorsed by a Lancashire League associate of later years. 'The reputation he had for being a clown was always superficial. What Johnny was really there for was to win. If he could get a laugh or two en route, that was fine by him.'

Wardle's humour was, more often than not, spiced with the wisdom of one of Shakespeare's Fools. Had he been at King Lear's side he would surely have prevented that sad old monarch from losing his reason. In cricket Wardle brought joy on a dull day, introducing a touch of irreverence when sobriety reigned.

Johnny did play the showman, especially to his own devoted gallery at Sheffield. But his fun at Bramall Lane and elsewhere demonstrated a masterly understanding of crowd psychology. He had an unerring grasp of the spectators' mood, whether he was moving in to bowl to the rhythms of a Johann Strauss polka – one, two, three, hop – as the brass band played at Scarborough, or lurching like a drunk with a bottle raised to his lips to avert a threatened riot in the West Indies. His humour was always spontaneous.

The comic antics were often employed to dissipate his own tension. 'I never made them happen; it was just that I saw something funny in a situation,' said Johnny. They also, one feels, presented a glimpse of a generous, warm man. 'Clowns cry,' says Trevor Bailey. The tears of an embattled cricketer were stifled by sympathetic laughter. As an entertainer, with wickets under his belt and the match won, the barricades were down. Johnny was at peace with the world and his friends – players and supporters – rejoiced in his tranquillity.

Geoff Cope, a younger Yorkshire cricketer, who hero-worshipped Wardle as a boy, came to realise why his idol was such an adored cricketer. 'It was because he was a top professional in every aspect of the game. When you are so good you can act the goat a bit.'

At the request of Don Wilson, Johnny's successor as Yorkshire's slow left-arm bowler, Wardle joined a county party on a tour of Bermuda in 1970. He was then aged 47. Keeping wicket to him in one game on the mat was the underestimated Jimmy Binks. Cope recalls:

> Johnny started to bowl his magic stuff – the mix of orthodox slows interspersed with the odd chinaman or googly. After two overs there were eight extras on the scoreboard. Johnny looked solemnly down the wicket and said: 'Binksie, you couldn't spot me when you started with Yorkshire and you still can't when I'm touching 50.'

Cope says the interlude ended with Wardle making matters easier for Binks. His signals included his handkerchief hanging out of his pocket for the chinaman and a scratch on the back of the head for the googly.

On the Bermuda trip Yorkshire played one match on a tiny ground nestling like a quarry in the countryside. Cope remembers: 'This brawny Bermudian hammered Johnny and myself for about 50 runs in 25 minutes. He lapped me. Johnny, who was fielding at square-leg, set off running. He must have run about 40 yards. In an acrobatic scramble, he dived forward into a somersault and exultantly threw his hand up. The batsman looked on with some amazement. Johnny shouted: "Go on, go, get off." ' A surge of applause greeted the Yorkshire veteran's athleticism.

The next batsman came out and took guard. Wardle moved up to the umpire who inquired: 'Any problems, John?' Wardle replied: 'Can I have your permission to leave the field?' The umpire asked for the reason. 'I'm going down the road to fetch the ball back,' said Johnny.

'Johnny had done everybody. He had not caught the ball. The batsman had belted it four fields away and no one had noticed, either on the field, or in the crowd,' says Cope. The wrongly dismissed batsman re-emerged from the pavilion. In his bemused state it was not surprising that his wickets were shattered off the first ball of the resumed innings.

Wardle's playful mood persisted throughout the game. Cope remembers that the next trick baffled one of his team-mates, Fred Trueman. 'Johnny had a magnificent sideways-on action and, as he bowled, he turned full tilt in his stride. The batsman played the ball back. Johnny, as he completed his follow-through, swivelled and called out to Trueman at mid-off: "Go on, Fred". Fred set off in hot pursuit of the ball. Suddenly, from the far distance, we heard him cry: "Where's the . . . . . . . ball?" ' By the end of Trueman's scamper to the boundary the batsmen were completing their fourth run. Johnny sported the widest of grins. 'All right, lads. Fred will soon get tired.' He then calmly pulled the ball from his pocket and quietly assured the umpire that he had taken a return catch.

Ted Lester describes another amusing incident, this time involving Wardle as the affronted player in a bridge game. In those days the Yorkshire team travelled by train to games. Lester was in one compartment and Wardle in another. 'I looked out and saw a pack of cards come flying out of the window.' He stepped down the corridor to make inquiries as to what had happened. Johnny was the culprit. He was red-faced with anger. He told Lester that he had been dealt so many bad hands that he had thrown out the cards in disgust. 'I'm not going to lose any more money,' he said.

One of Jim Laker's favourite Wardle stories concerned Johnny going out to face Ray Lindwall for the first time. 'I was so nervous, I could not keep my bat still as I took guard,' related Wardle. Frank Chester, the umpire, at length lost patience with the dithering Johnny. He demanded: 'Now, come on, what *do* you want?' Wardle replied: 'A slow full toss down the legside, please.'

The hallowed environs of Lord's did not escape Johnny's jests. Cricket's elder statesman, former England captain Gubby Allen, has another memory of the humour which refused to be quenched, even in a Test match. 'Johnny holed out in front of the Grandstand. The fieldsman threw it back. Johnny was just turning towards the pavilion. He was a left-handed batsman and the ball bounced invitingly beside him. He pivoted on his heels and struck the ball full-pitch in to the crowd.' Allen says others thought it was a little naughty and rather bad behaviour. 'But it was extremely funny; he did it so nicely, with such a friendly smile, and everybody laughed.'

The late Bill Bowes remembered another Test occasion at Lord's when Wardle stopped the clatter of typewriters in the press box. Rarely had he laughed more at the antics of a player on a cricket field. Keith Miller, the Australian bowler, bowling at his fastest, made a ball lift from a good length to hit Johnny on his thigh. It was a painful blow, but Johnny moved back from his stumps and vigorously rubbed his elbow. In his next over Miller unleashed a bumper which struck Wardle right on the point of the elbow. His response was to limp away and massage his knee even more vigorously. By this time Miller was rubbing his own sides with laughter. 'In the circumstances, I wondered how Keith could be expected to bowl on target,' said Bowes. 'He couldn't and he was still chuckling when he delivered his next ball. It was very, very wide.'

Peter May presents another delightful anecdote from the 1953–4 tour of the West Indies. It occurred during a drinks halt in one game on the mat in Trinidad. Two late order batsmen, both extremely nervous, were at the wicket when the refreshments were brought out. They were only too pleased to take a break and laid down their bats before joining the huddle of players. 'This little chap scuttled over to get his drink. When he turned his back Johnny picked up his bat and tucked it under the mat at the far end.' The merriment of the crowd, who had watched Johnny's prank, increased as the batsman searched in vain for his missing bat. Eventually Wardle gave his opponent a consoling pat on the back, retrieved the bat, and allowed him to continue his innings.

Frank Tyson considers that Johnny's humour was of the quiet brand, intended to astonish rather than cause uproarious laughter. He recalls an occasion when the MCC team were playing golf at the Glenelg Club in Adelaide. Wardle was a member of one of the last foursomes into the clubhouse, the lounge of which was on a hill overlooking the eighteenth green.

> Johnny hooked his approach shot to the green and it landed with a clatter on the concave corrugated iron roof of the building. The '19th' hole was crowded and all its occupants were amazed when Johnny appeared in front of the large lounge windows with a ladder which he propped against the roof and gravely mounted with a nine-iron in his hand. He climbed the ladder and disappeared from view. Moments

later there was the noise of a club head striking the roof and the ball lobbed on to the green to finish inches from the pin. The shot was greeted with loud applause. We did not find out until later that Johnny had hit the roof with the club and thrown the ball on to the green!

Bright cricket by day and convivial evenings at Scarborough linger in the memory of Godfrey Evans. Evans, less vigilant than usual following an extra round of nightcaps, was hiccuping next morning in one festival game. 'I misread Johnny's googly for the chinaman and it went for four byes.' 'Hurray', shouted Johnny, 'I've done you at last.' Evans says Wardle was unsurpassed in his experience as a cricket entertainer. He provides another cameo of the buoyant Johnny at Scarborough. 'I was bowling my "flat spin and gin" and Johnny gave an absolutely first-class impersonation of me behind the stumps. For a quarter of an hour he had the team and the spectators in fits of laughter.'

Wardle, in the words of R. C. Robertson Glasgow, proved that conjuring and cricket were first cousins. He had a highly developed ball sense, the product of his days as a footballer. In one game in Australia he brought off a freak catch at mid-wicket. The ball was hit high and wide. Wardle jumped and managed to tip the ball with his right hand above his head. As the ball hovered in the air, he nodded it into his hands. His old soccer manager, Major Frank Buckley, would have appreciated this deft touch. Wardle's footwork, too, had the dexterity of a music-hall juggler. One of his favourite tricks was to trap the ball with his feet, flick it upwards and catch it behind his back.

Johnny's brand of cricket 'kidology' vastly amused his followers. It also drove his batting rivals wild with distraction. The frolics, said Wardle, were really paraded to ease his own tension. 'The batsmen thought I wasn't trying and the crowd loved it; it was a combination of things; and I had a happy knack of being able to do it at the right time.' Godfrey Evans considers that a lot of Johnny's fun on the field had a serious purpose, since it was designed to sap the batsman's concentration. As a cover fieldsman, Wardle would run alongside a hard-driven ball, stop it, then pretend, very convincingly, that he had missed it and start to gallop off in the opposite direction. Less alert batsmen would start to run and then have to dash back as Johnny feigned to throw at the wicket. At other times Wardle would pounce on the ball, slip it quickly from one hand to the other, and reverse the direction of his throw. So great would be the batsmen's confusion as to Johnny's intention, that they might both be running to the wrong end.

On two occasions Wardle used the same trick to fool his opponents. He first played the joke on Michael Barton, the Surrey captain, in a match at the Oval. He related:

> I was fielding at short-leg to Alec Coxon. Alec bowled a long hop and Barton whoofed it. I saw it all the way, stuck my left hand out, and it was in. As I caught it, I turned round. Geoffrey Keighley was on the boundary. A grand lad, Geoffrey. He was an upright runner, with a high knee action. At the Oval, when you're on the boundary, you very rarely see the ball until it is half-way to you. I pointed and called out: 'Over there, Geoffrey.' He set off at a tremendous gallop. And, bugger me, when I looked back, Barton was coming back for two. The other batsman had seen what had happened, and he told his skipper: 'He's caught it'. That were him, and I wasn't too popular for making the captain look daft.

Cyril Washbrook was the victim of the same trick at Sheffield.

> He hit the ball like a shell. It went straight to me, one hand, and I caught it. Washie was running for two, possibly three. He was proper upset and disgusted was Washie, because I'd made him look so silly.

Wardle especially relished his duels with the great Lancastrian. In another Roses game Johnny had stepped up to deliver his wristy off-spinner three or four times. Washbrook, in near disdain, had pushed comfortably to the onside of the field for runs. Up came Wardle again, with the same chinaman action, and Washbrook positioned himself for an easy push to leg. Too late he found the ball spinning the other way, and instead of pushing it wide of mid-on, he hit the ball straight back to the bowler. Johnny caught it and chuckled with delight at his deception.

Another cunning coup was achieved against another Lancashire rival, Alan Wharton.

> It was one of my best wickets. Alan was coming up to his century. He liked to pull a lot and I said to Ted Lester, who was fielding out at deep square-leg: 'Just move around every ball and keep moving until my fourth ball. Then I'll want you to move bloody quickly just in front of square. But make sure that when Alan looks back, after each ball, that you are where you ought to be.'

Johnny had set his trap for a deliberate long hop. 'I knew that Wharton wouldn't fall for it if I didn't disguise my intention.' As he ran up to bowl, Johnny pretended to slip as he delivered the ball.

'Alan fell for it and holed out, as intended to Lester. As he passed me, he said: "I should have had more ........ sense." Whoof, bang, and he was out.' As Johnny said, it was a cheeky wicket. He did not mind his rivals pondering on his impudence when they were having a cigarette back in the pavilion.

It was this irresistible cheekiness, steering just clear of outrage, which is remembered by men now in ripe middle age. They formed the legions of admiring small boys for whom Johnny Wardle was the adventurous Peter Pan figure in his soaring flights of imagination on the cricket field. For all his greatness he was a child at heart: his essential good fun was perhaps his happiest legacy.

'He didn't have to do much as an entertainer,' says Godfrey Evans. 'What he did was so funny.'

# 12
# Visions in Retirement

> 'Everyone shared in the enjoyment when Johnny Wardle played cricket. He left no one in any doubt that he was a Yorkshireman and that here was a man prepared to accept any challenge.' – Mike Cowan.

THERE was sadness and joy in the last years of Johnny Wardle's life. His vigorous lifestyle encompassed new sporting triumphs as a golfer; there was the remarkable transformation of a primitive shanty site, the unkempt acres of fishponds and ramshackle sheds, in South Yorkshire into a convivial country club and cricket school; his acclaimed work as a groundsman at Doncaster; and his renaissance as a cricket philosopher and guide. He was a visionary and resourceful man whose belatedly recognised qualities at last burst through in his reconciliation with the Yorkshire cricket hierarchy.

It was a long haul back to forgiveness, effected in the 1970s by his election as an honorary life member of the county club. When he was finally given this accolade and the sanctuary so long denied him, two members of the Yorkshire committee offered their congratulations. 'It was the worst thing we ever did when we got rid of you, lad,' they told Johnny.

The catalyst for the reunion was probably Wardle's association – a bond resembling a father-and-son relationship – with Geoff Cope, the Yorkshire off-spinner. So strong was their accord that Cope was the only mourner outside the family to be allowed to send flowers when Wardle died in July, 1985. He inscribed the card attached to his wreath with the words: 'To Dad.'

Wardle, the cricket outcast of a generation before, was given the task of remodelling Cope's action when the young bowler was banned from first-class cricket in 1972. Cope was advised: 'Go and see Wardle. You'll see a hero.'

Cope remembers his feelings of awe at going to see his boyhood idol. 'The success of our relationship is that from the first day of our meeting I had respect for the man.' He went to Wardle's cricket school in a mood of deep depression. His cricket career was in tatters. At Thorne he experienced one of those rare, liberating moments of contentment. 'If we succeed, you've succeeded,' said Johnny. 'If we fail, we've failed.' The wild man of legend no longer existed. 'Here was a warm man,' says Cope, 'with his arm around you and saying: "come on pal, we can do it".' On the first day – the prelude to a long, arduous spell of tuition – the two men, master and pupil, drank coffee and talked and talked as the clock ticked on. At the end of the day Wardle told the Yorkshire bowler: 'If we do this right, Geoff, you'll play for England.'

Cope recalls: 'There was a hole in the ground; it was six feet deep; and I was halfway down it. And he was saying to me: "You'll *play for England*." ' Wardle's prophecy seemed to belong to the realms of fantasy to the young Yorkshireman pitched in gloom. But it was fulfilled, after months of painstaking, concentrated practice and minor matches away from critical scrutiny but under the eye of Wardle's camera in league cricket. In the winter of 1976–7 Cope was a member of the MCC party which toured India and Sri Lanka, and in the following year he played in three Tests in Pakistan under Mike Brearley's captaincy.

On the morning after his preliminary discussion with Wardle, Cope again drove out to Thorne. Johnny completely reshaped Cope's action, showing him how to do it as a 'right-handed Wardle'. In the first three weeks of the course Cope could not even hit the green mat of the wicket at the cricket school. As the months went by the pieces gradually started to assemble in his sporting puzzle. 'Suddenly it all started to click; the rhythm and the control returned; and there was a big kick up the backside from Johnny.' Wardle was a hard taskmaster. He revealed a different side to his character when Cope began to attain a measure of proficiency. 'When we first met Johnny was a kind of cuddly bear; but now he became a raging lion as he urged me on to greater effort. What was magic about Johnny was that everything he asked you to do he could do himself.'

Cope returned to first-class cricket with Yorkshire against Nottinghamshire at Bramall Lane, Sheffield in August, 1973.

> It was a tremendous day. I came on to bowl at the bottom end. I could only see one face in the old stand. That was Wardle. He just kept looking, very intently, at me. As I turned back he was encouraging me in dumb show – thumbs up and hand actions.

Cope estimates that he bowled around 20 overs on that day at Sheffield. Wardle, he thinks, as the protective and anxious onlooker, mentally bowled double that number. 'He was very tired at the end of the day,' says Cope.

In one league game, before Cope's return to first-class cricket, Wardle was filming his pupil. At the end of one over there was a shout from the rim of the field. 'Geoff', called out an enraged Johnny. 'Come here, I want to talk to you. You've just bowled four overs at that feller. He can't play on the leg-side at all. Yet there you are pumping away at his off-stump. Come on, start thinking about the game.' Cope returned to the middle and the umpire remarked: 'Is he going?' 'I don't think so,' replied Cope. 'But I might be if I don't buck my ideas up.'

Cope, as a result of this and other uncompromising lessons by Wardle, took more first-class wickets than anyone else in the country in 1976. 'Dad,' he says, 'was the type of person I would have liked to have seen in the Yorkshire dressing-room because the kids would have learned so much from him.' Some of these boys, one of whom, Arthur Robinson, still marvels at Johnny's acumen, were introduced to the great man during a match at Abbeydale Park, Sheffield. Wardle said to Robinson: 'Pleased to meet you, lad. I could put two yards of pace on you.' Robinson, as an accurate but unstartling seam bowler, was puzzled and intrigued by the remark. 'Do you think he would help me?' he asked Cope. An impromptu coaching session, lasting only 15 minutes, was arranged with Wardle. In explanation of the subsequent events Cope says that 'Rocker', as he was known in the Yorkshire dressing-room, Brian Bolus, the Derbyshire opening batsman, and himself were members of a club called the Saints.

Bolus went out to bat for Derbyshire twenty minutes before the close of play. Robinson was one of Yorkshire's opening bowlers. 'Rocker bounced Bolly,' recalls Cope. 'He was half forward, half "what's this", and he ended up with both legs coming off the ground, his head tucked between his knees, and down on his bottom.' Cope was fielding at forward short-leg. 'Rocker had a big grin on his face. Bolly looked down at him and said: "Arthur, that was not a very saintly thing to do." ' The Yorkshire fieldsmen were as amazed as Bolus himself at Robinson's unprecedented burst of speed. Wardle, in the shade of the sponsors' tent, looked up and roared with laughter at the disbelief of both batsman and fieldsmen.

Geoff Cope himself, as a legatee of Wardle's wiles, was able to earn the respect of England captain Mike Brearley in a Test match against Pakistan. Cope remembers how Johnny had told him that he should always deploy his four best fieldsmen in the four most important positions. This information was relayed to Brearley when Cope insisted on a drastically altered field setting for his bowling. Brearley, as he responded to the rearrangement, sported a smile of recognition. 'Your adviser didn't happen to be a certain well-known slow left-arm bowler?' he asked.

For one opponent, inclined to play with an open-faced bat, the England captain installed a gully for Cope against the Yorkshire bowler's wishes. The fourth ball of the over looped gently upwards via the batsman's bat and pads. Brearley's gully fieldsman dived forward but was a foot short of making the catch. Brearley walked straight up the wicket to Cope and said: 'I will never interfere again. Sorry, I've cost you your first Test wicket.' After that mishap Brearley's sole instructions to Cope were: 'I'd like to attack or defend.' Cope was allowed to set the field he wanted. Brearley knew that if Cope was satisfied with the field placings he would do his best for him and the team.

Edna Wardle was the unswerving, if at times, reluctant partner in her husband's activities. She was more than a little dismayed during the exchange of her 'lovely Victorian house' at Wakefield for the mud, sweat and tears of the business venture at Thorne. She remembers how they had ploughed the proceeds of Johnny's Yorkshire benefit – a figure severely eroded by the county's management of the money – into the business.

Ever since the days of Lord Hawke's stewardship Yorkshire had invested the cash of beneficiaries, mainly as a guard against the improvidence of players but also as a security for their wives. A sum of £6,000 (out of a total of £8,000) was released by the Yorkshire committee after discussions and an investigation of the Wardles' venture. But around £1,000 had been lost in a swift and unforeseen slump in the county's investment. Afterwards Johnny wryly commented: 'If it's my brass, I would rather have lost it myself.'

It was a financial loss of some consequence but Johnny and Edna weathered the blow in characteristically hard-working style. In the beginning at Thorne there was a small cottage, three large fishponds and a few outbuildings. Attached to the cottage was a shop where the Wardles sold innumerable cups of tea and fried egg sandwiches, a particular favourite of the fishermen visitors. A selection of the escapades of a daunting enterprise would yield material for a television comedy series. The Wardles were involved in an hilarious sprawl of mishaps, with Buster, the family dog, galloping to the fore as a character quite as strong and incorrigible as his master and mistress. Edna and Johnny were 'do-it-yourself' pioneers on a gigantic scale. It was a rough passage to success and the Wardles seemed to thrive on making things as hard as possible for themselves. Edna's, if not Johnny's, nerves were stretched to screaming point at times.

One of her chores was to fill the anglers' tins with different sized maggots. The evil-smelling bait was kept in an old tin bath in an outbuilding. One day Edna went to refill the tins. She opened the door to discover a seething mass of maggots wriggling in ecstasy on the floor. Rain had dripped through a leak in the roof and into the bath. Edna, in a blazing temper, swept the escapist maggots back into the container. Of this and other adventures she says: 'You can get used to anything in time.' After her initial distress, she became the proud assessor of the supplies of maggots. 'My, these maggots are grand this week. They're so fat and juicy,' she would say.

On another occasion, when the fishermen complained about the weed-infested ponds, Edna and Johnny hired a van, tied a wire rope to it, and loosened the weeds in the ponds with a farmer's harrow attached to the rope. Great mounds of black sludge were hauled from the pond with rakes. 'I remember standing one day with Johnny as we pulled out the weeds. It was so heavy and you could only take out a little at a time.' The tears streamed down Edna's face as she looked at the heap of weed. The mass showed no signs of getting smaller. She told Johnny: 'This is like trying to empty the sea with a teaspoon.' Johnny wearily replied: 'Just make your mind a blank and keep going.'

The proximity of the ponds to their cottage also brought the problem of rats. One day Edna, to her astonishment, revealed powers of marksmanship to place her as a contender to Annie Oakley. Johnny gave her a gun, instructed her in its use, and told her to mount guard in the kitchen. 'I had never held a gun in my life. I was baking and it was very quiet. I didn't have to wait long. The back door was slightly ajar and the rat appeared.' Edna pulled the trigger and hit it. She squirmed at the squeal of the wounded rat but ran up to the pond, rejoicing at her triumph. 'Johnny,' she cried, 'I hit it.' It was her first and only confrontation with the rats. Having made one conquest, she decided that discretion was the better part of valour.

The arrival of a cavalcade of gypsies at Thorne was in the best traditions of a Wild West movie. Johnny was away on cricket duty in Lancashire when the band of gypsies pitched their luxury caravans on the site. Edna, thinking to supplement the family income, had acceded to their request to park the caravans on the land for three weeks. She thought Johnny would be pleased at her initiative. She charged the visitors a rental of £10 a week. It preceded what amounted to a take-over. The gypsies made themselves thoroughly at home. The lights of the caravans at night blazed as if in a fairground. The screech of radios made sleep impossible.

Alsatian dogs prowled menacingly around the area. Buster, the Wardles' own dog, was perplexed and confused at the invasion of his domain. The fishermen were similarly cowed by the intruders and stayed away. Johnny's reaction when he returned home can safely be left to the imagination. He had to enlist the aid of a policeman friend to persuade the gypsies – a burly and forbidding regiment – and their hordes of children to make their departures. 'We had many a good laugh about it afterwards,' says Edna. 'But it wasn't so funny at the time. I feared for Johnny – the gypsies had the build of all-in wrestlers – and I was glad to come out of that episode without any broken bones.'

As the Wardles inched their way to prosperity and the homespun fishermen's cafe became the Ponderosa Country Club, Johnny was able to devote more time to golf, a sporting pursuit which had first claimed his attention on cricket tours. He was to become an outstanding golfer, playing consistently to a handicap of two, and displaying the same professionalism which he had brought to his cricket. He was captain of the Wheatley Golf Club at Doncaster in 1977 and chairman of the Green Committee for five years. In 1978, at the age of 55 and in his first year as a senior, Johnny won the Yorkshire County Seniors' Amateur Championship. Three years later he was again the victor in the tournament.

Edna Wardle, at first a sceptic and resentful of her husband's prolonged absences at golf, grew in time to become as passionate about the sport as Johnny. He was overjoyed by her enthusiasm and they later shared many successes in local tournaments. 'I became so keen on golf that I thought it was a waste of time going home,' recalls Edna. 'Johnny played with the men and I played with the women. I would then be waiting for him so that we could play together.' The Wheatley members would say to her: 'Edna, you're going to wear him out.'

As the unpaid groundsman at the Wheatley Golf Club and later at the Doncaster Town Cricket Club, Wardle brought the accumulated knowledge of many years to bear in transforming these sporting surfaces. His persistent and tenacious work at the two clubs brought other lasting memorials to his talents. 'Johnny enjoyed being involved with the work of the Green staff,' says Ken Percival, the Wheatley club secretary. 'There was nothing he liked better than to enjoy the fresh air from the seat of a tractor with a set of gang mowers behind him.' Edna Wardle remembers the long days spent by her husband at the club. 'He worked for nothing, just did it for love. The greens were absolutely fantastic, like lightning. He would stay up at the club all hours.'

Shortly before his death Wardle, the ground expert, inveighed against the introduction of heavy loam in the search for quicker cricket wickets.

> It is very difficult soil to work with, water will not penetrate it, neither will the grass roots which are so vital to binding it together. The wicket cracks both vertically and horizontally, resulting in uneven bounce. Batsmen are having to wear helmets and other protective clothing. Never mind what anyone says, all the great players of the past would have needed protection had they played under these conditions.

Wardle said that medium-paced bowling had replaced spinners because it was harder to play on modern wickets with their uneven bounce.

> The old-fashioned slower wickets used to dust a little and help only the spinner and were never dangerous. The ordinary medium pacer came in for some hammer. One had to be pretty quick, with some swing, or slow with plenty of spin and flight to succeed.

There were trenchant words, too, on the covering of wickets, which was temporarily abandoned in 1986.

> The captain with four or five fast bowlers has no need to worry about the weather. I wonder what the averages of some batsmen would be like if they had to face Laker, Lock, Appleyard and Underwood on rain-affected wickets. Even the great Viv Richards would be brought back to earth with a bang.

The heart of Wardle's argument was that spectators had been denied the sight of one of the beauties of the game – the artistry of the spin bowler.

Johnny Wardle's skills were unveiled again in his twilight years. He was cajoled out of retirement to play in two other cricket matches, one in his fifties for Nelson, and the other for the Minor Counties Nomads just a year before he died. The Nelson club persuaded him, against his better judgement, to deputise for their injured professional. Geoff Cope remembers meeting Johnny on the Monday morning following the Nelson match. He had heard Wardle's protestations that he was too old to return to Lancashire League cricket. Johnny complained of stiffness as he and Cope walked round the grounds of the club at Thorne. 'Ah went over to Nelson to play for them. I shouldn't have done it,' said Wardle. 'I got 5 for 40 and scored 46 not out. Nay, you just put it there and they get themselves out.' An impish grin spread over his face. 'My figures should have been 6 for 30. They're not as good a fielding side as they used to be. I had to have a few words with one or two of them in the field.'

At the age of 61, Wardle travelled down to Wallingford in Oxfordshire, ostensibly to umpire and present prizes in a match between the local club and the Minor Counties eleven. He could not resist the opportunity of another bowling spell. It was the last glimpse of the master at work. The run-up was graceful and smooth and the ball pitched unerringly on a length. He took 7 wickets for 50 runs in 19 overs to dismiss Wallingford for 178. As someone said: 'How can a man bowl like that and entertain in a style that has Chaplinesque humour?' These words could have served as Wardle's epitaph.

The first symptoms of the illness which was to end the life of this special man were bouts of dizziness and a lack of co-ordination. Geoff Cope, who drove home with Wardle after a dinner at the Baildon Cricket Club, remembers his anxiety. 'I was very worried. Johnny was not well at all.' It had, for all that, been an evening of splendid cricket talk, with Wardle in a happy mood. The planned after-dinner speeches were forgotten as Johnny suddenly launched into a coaching session. The jokes were replaced by questions and answers. Johnny left his seat at the top table and wandered round the guests, making one earnest point after another in an unforgettable debate.

In February 1985 Wardle visited the Yorkshire cricket headquarters at Headingley to finalise the terms of his new contract as bowling consultant with the county club. He was due to take up the appointment on 1 March. Sid Fielden, the Yorkshire public relations chairman, drove Wardle to Headingley. 'People noticed that Johnny had been confused during the day, except when he was talking about cricket,' remembers Fielden. Wardle had regaled the local press corps with a fund of stories. He bubbled over with enthusiasm as he talked about his plans to revive Yorkshire cricket. His presence, in the words of one of the reporters, was like a breath of fresh air sweeping the ground. But Johnny was tired after this exciting day. On his return home he staggered and bumped against a wall after leaving Fielden's car.

Edna Wardle remembers Johnny's aberrations at this time. 'There was a monster getting at his brain. He was not behaving normally. I thought he was having a nervous breakdown.' An ear specialist was called in to prescribe treatment for the dizziness, but the illness persisted. On some days Johnny, the 'workaholic', was affected by a strange lethargy. He would lie down and rest on the sofa.

In April Wardle underwent an operation to remove a brain tumour. Before the operation at the Sheffield Royal Hallamshire Hospital he was asked by his family if he was frightened about the outcome of the surgery. 'Am I buggered?' he said. 'After this is done I shall be a changed man. I will smile at you all and give you a pound out of the till.'

Although he was a sick man, Johnny's humour never entirely deserted him. Edna Wardle recalls visiting her husband in hospital. The floor around his bed was sprayed with orange juice. 'It's to make the nurse feel more at home,' was Johnny's explanation. 'I didn't know what he meant,' says Edna. 'But I did when she came along the ward. She was a Jamaican girl.'

Wardle, at first, seemed to be making a good recovery after the operation. Sid Fielden remembers taking his friend to Headingley for the last time to watch part of a match at the beginning of the season. 'Johnny wore his England blazer and signed autographs as we walked round the ground.' At home, during his short reprieve, Johnny was even well enough to practise golf shots on the garden lawn.

Sadly, the illness took a hold again. Edna Wardle recalls one of the last of the happy times she and Johnny spent together. They walked down to the village newsagent to buy a football paper. On the way home they collected two packs of Chinese food for supper. The meal has a special poignancy for Edna. Beside the kitchen table their remembrances glowed in a swell of affection. 'Johnny gave me a kiss and said: "You know that I love you, don't you, Edna?" I felt as if I was 17 again. That was the last time that Johnny was truly in charge of himself.'

On the first Christmas after his death she picked out at random a page from her store of Johnny's letters. 'Although I am not with you in person, I am with you in spirit,' was the message in Johnny's bold handwriting on the page.

Johnny Wardle, a fine ambassador for Yorkshire cricket, was a stern defender of the old-fashioned principles of integrity passed on to him by such mentors as Brian Sellers, Maurice Leyland and Bill Bowes. 'If you're chosen to play for Yorkshire, you work to deserve that honour, every single minute of the day,' he once said. 'You have only a short career, it's not a long time to give of your best and be paid for something you enjoy doing.'

One of his friends during his later years as a cricket adjudicator was Glen Emanuel, the National Westminster Bank campaign manager. Emanuel says:

> Johnny was straight, honest and a gentle man behind the craggy Yorkshire exterior. I always found him cheerful company. He enjoyed a laugh, loved his cricket and commanded the respect not only of his peers but among lesser mortals like myself.

In South Yorkshire, which always remained his spiritual home, Johnny used his prestige as a cricketer to bring nation-wide recognition to his local cricket society at Wombwell. He was the first winner of the society's annual Cricketer of the Year award. In appreciation of his efforts, the Wombwell society has recently introduced the Johnny Wardle Memorial Award which will be presented annually for the best individual bowling performance in South Yorkshire League cricket.

'Everyone shared in the enjoyment when Johnny Wardle played cricket,' said former Yorkshire fast bowler, Mike Cowan, in his funeral address at the 700-year-old church of St Lawrence at Hatfield Woodhouse, near Doncaster. 'He left no one in any doubt that he was a Yorkshireman. His set jaw, the broad shoulders and strong forearms all portrayed the fact that here was a man prepared to accept any challenge.'

The deep wells of wisdom of a cricket giant remained untapped, abruptly sealed by Wardle's untimely death. Edna Wardle believes that Yorkshire made amends for their neglect by placing Johnny back at the top of their class. 'His appointment as bowling coach was the crowning glory. The fact that he was sadly unable to carry out the task did not matter.' But the recognition came too late and the regrets of a saddened county will never erase the futility of his exclusion and the waste of a towering talent.

# Statistical Appendices

## J. H. WARDLE
## In First-Class Cricket 1946–68
## Compiled by Roy D. Wilkinson

Debut for Yorkshire: v Worcestershire at Leeds, 20 July 1946
Last match for Yorkshire: v Somerset at Sheffield, 1 August 1958

Debut for England: v West Indies at Port-of-Spain, 11 February 1948
Last match for England: v West Indies at Lord's, 22 June 1957

Last first-class match: President's XI v Prime Minister's XI at Bombay, 9 April 1968 (Koyna Relief Fund Match)

### BATTING AND FIELDING

| Season | M. | I. | N.O. | Runs | H.S. | Avge. | 50's | Century P'ships | Catches |
|---|---|---|---|---|---|---|---|---|---|
| 1946 | 1 | 2 | 2 | 12 | 10* | – | – | – | – |
| 1947 | 24 | 36 | 4 | 582 | 63* | 18.18 | 2 | – | 24 |
| 1947–8 (West Indies) | 6 | 8 | 1 | 77 | 35 | 11.00 | – | – | 2 |
| 1948 | 31 | 34 | 6 | 466 | 40* | 16.64 | – | – | 29 |
| 1949 | 21 | 28 | 4 | 412 | 70 | 17.16 | 2 | 1 | 15 |
| 1950 | 33 | 47 | 8 | 733 | 59* | 18.79 | 2 | – | 24 |
| 1951 | 34 | 39 | 2 | 612 | 79 | 16.54 | 2 | 2 | 20 |
| 1952 | 36 | 47 | 8 | 683 | 50 | 17.51 | 1 | – | 20 |
| 1953 | 31 | 42 | 9 | 580 | 43 | 17.57 | – | – | 19 |
| 1953–4 (West Indies) | 5 | 5 | – | 130 | 66 | 26.00 | 1 | 1 | 5 |
| 1954 | 32 | 38 | 3 | 537 | 72 | 15.34 | 4 | – | 24 |
| 1954–5 (Australia) | 14 | 18 | 2 | 291 | 63 | 18.18 | 1 | 1 | 6 |
| 1954–5 (New Zealand) | 4 | 5 | 1 | 50 | 32* | 12.50 | – | – | 3 |
| 1955 | 34 | 47 | 1 | 571 | 74 | 12.41 | 1 | – | 17 |
| 1956 | 35 | 41 | 6 | 526 | 55* | 15.02 | 1 | – | 22 |
| 1956–7 (South Africa) | 14 | 18 | 3 | 207 | 37 | 13.80 | – | – | 11 |
| 1957 | 32 | 42 | 7 | 546 | 64 | 15.60 | 1 | – | 9 |
| 1958 | 24 | 28 | 4 | 303 | 42 | 12.62 | – | – | 7 |
| 1967–8 (India) | 1 | 2 | – | 15 | 14 | 7.50 | – | – | – |
| Totals | 412 | 527 | 71 | 7333 | 79 | 16.08 | 18 | 5 | 257 |

Statistical Appendices 159

## BOWLING

| Season | M. | Overs | Mdns. | Runs | Wkts. | Avge. | Runs per 100 Balls | Wkts per 100 Balls | 5 wkts in an Inns | 10 wkts in a Match |
|---|---|---|---|---|---|---|---|---|---|---|
| 1946 | 1 | 3 | 0 | 10 | 0 | – | 55.55 | – | – | – |
| 1947 | 24 | 992 | 362 | 2190 | 86 | 25.46 | 36.79 | 1.44 | 4 | – |
| 1947–8 (West Indies) | 6 | 171.5 | 34 | 441 | 6 | 73.50 | 42.77 | 0.58 | – | – |
| 1948 | 31 | 1303.4 | 483 | 2923 | 150 | 19.48 | 37.36 | 1.91 | 12 | 2 |
| 1949 | 21 | 1093.1 | 407 | 2333 | 103 | 22.65 | 35.56 | 1.57 | 12 | 5 |
| 1950 | 33 | 1638.5 | 741 | 2909 | 174 | 16.71 | 29.58 | 1.76 | 14 | 1 |
| 1951 | 34 | 1375 | 616 | 2504 | 127 | 19.71 | 30.35 | 1.53 | 6 | 1 |
| 1952 | 36 | 1847.2 | 810 | 3460 | 177 | 19.54 | 31.21 | 1.59 | 18 | 3 |
| 1953 | 31 | 1606.2 | 601 | 3540 | 146 | 24.24 | 36.72 | 1.51 | 10 | 4 |
| 1953–4 (West Indies) | 5 | 240.3 | 77 | 569 | 18 | 31.61 | 39.43 | 1.24 | 1 | – |
| 1954 | 32 | 1262 | 520 | 2449 | 155 | 15.80 | 32.34 | 2.04 | 13 | 2 |
| 1954–5 (Australia) | 14 | 269.7† | 61 | 832 | 37 | 22.48 | 38.53 | 1.71 | 2 | – |
| 1954–5 (New Zealand) | 4 | 165.4 | 74 | 334 | 20 | 16.70 | 33.60 | 2.01 | 1 | – |
| 1955 | 34 | 1496.4 | 572 | 3149 | 195 | 16.14 | 35.06 | 2.17 | 13 | 2 |
| 1956 | 35 | 1241.1 | 466 | 2482 | 153 | 16.22 | 33.32 | 2.05 | 8 | 1 |
| 1956–7 (South Africa) | 14 | 380.3† | 94 | 1103 | 90 | 12.25 | 36.24 | 2.95 | 8 | 4 |
| 1957 | 32 | 1047.4 | 403 | 2281 | 114 | 20.00 | 36.28 | 1.81 | 7 | 2 |
| 1958 | 24 | 716.4 | 281 | 1401 | 91 | 15.39 | 32.58 | 2.11 | 5 | 2 |
| 1967–8 (India) | 1 | 34.4 | 4 | 117 | 4 | 29.25 | 56.25 | 1.92 | – | – |
| Totals | 412 | 16236.1 / 650.2† | 6606 | 35027 | 1846 | 18.97 | 34.13 | 1.79 | 134 | 29 |

†8 ball overs

## TEST MATCHES
### BATTING AND FIELDING

| Season | M. | I. | N.O. | Runs | H.S. | Avge. | 50's | Century P'ships | Catches |
|---|---|---|---|---|---|---|---|---|---|
| 1947–8 v West Indies | 1 | 2 | 1 | 6 | 4 | 6.00 | – | – | – |
| 1950 v West Indies | 1 | 2 | 1 | 54 | 33* | 54.00 | – | – | – |
| 1951 v South Africa | 2 | 3 | – | 53 | 30 | 17.66 | – | – | – |
| 1953 v Australia | 3 | 4 | 2 | 57 | 29* | 28.50 | – | – | – |
| 1953–4 v West Indies | 2 | 2 | – | 104 | 66 | 52.00 | 1 | 1 | 2 |
| 1954 v Pakistan | 4 | 5 | 1 | 88 | 54 | 22.00 | 1 | – | 6 |
| 1954–5 v Australia | 4 | 6 | 1 | 109 | 38 | 21.80 | – | – | 1 |
| 1954–5 v New Zealand | 2 | 2 | 1 | 32 | 32* | 32.00 | – | – | – |
| 1955 v South Africa | 3 | 5 | – | 71 | 24 | 14.20 | – | – | – |
| 1956 v Australia | 1 | 2 | – | 0 | 0 | 0.00 | – | – | – |
| 1956–7 v South Africa | 4 | 7 | 1 | 68 | 22 | 11.33 | – | – | 3 |
| 1957 v West Indies | 1 | 1 | – | 11 | 11 | 11.00 | – | – | – |
| Totals | 28 | 41 | 8 | 653 | 66 | 19.78 | 2 | 1 | 12 |

## Statistical Appendices

## BOWLING

| Season | M. | Overs | Mdns. | Runs | Wkts. | Avge. | Runs Per 100 Balls | Wkts Per 100 Balls | 5 Wkts in an Inns | 10 Wkts in an Match |
|---|---|---|---|---|---|---|---|---|---|---|
| 1947–8 v West Indies | 1 | 3 | 0 | 9 | 0 | – | 50.00 | – | – | – |
| 1950 v West Indies | 1 | 47 | 16 | 104 | 2 | 52.00 | 36.87 | 0.70 | – | – |
| 1951 v South Africa | 2 | 95.5 | 39 | 171 | 5 | 34.20 | 29.73 | 0.86 | – | – |
| 1953 v Australia | 3 | 155.3 | 57 | 344 | 13 | 26.46 | 36.87 | 1.39 | – | – |
| 1953–4 v West Indies | 2 | 83.3 | 23 | 187 | 4 | 46.75 | 37.32 | 0.79 | – | – |
| 1954 v Pakistan | 4 | 142.5 | 82 | 176 | 20 | 8.80 | 20.53 | 2.33 | 1 | – |
| 1954–5 v Australia | 4 | 70.6† | 15 | 229 | 10 | 22.90 | 40.45 | 1.76 | 1 | – |
| 1954–5 v New Zealand | 2 | 76.3 | 43 | 116 | 5 | 23.20 | 25.27 | 1.08 | – | – |
| 1955 v South Africa | 3 | 165.4 | 77 | 273 | 15 | 18.20 | 27.46 | 1.50 | – | – |
| 1956 v Australia | 1 | 27 | 9 | 59 | 1 | 59.00 | 36.41 | 0.61 | – | – |
| 1956–7 v South Africa | 4 | 139.6† | 37 | 359 | 26 | 13.80 | 32.11 | 2.32 | 3 | 1 |
| 1957 v West Indies | 1 | 22 | 5 | 53 | 1 | 53.00 | 40.15 | 0.75 | – | – |
| Totals | 28 | 210.4†<br>818.5 | 403 | 2080 | 102 | 20.39 | 31.52 | 1.54 | 5 | 1 |

†8 ball overs

## FOR YORKSHIRE – COUNTY CHAMPIONSHIP
## BOWLING

| Yorkshire versus | M. | Overs | Mdns. | Runs | Wkts. | Avge. | Runs Per 100 Balls | Wkts. Per 100 Balls | 5 Wkts in an Inns | 10 Wkts in a Match |
|---|---|---|---|---|---|---|---|---|---|---|
| Derbyshire | 18 | 788.5 | 359 | 1400 | 58 | 24.56 | 29.57 | 1.22 | 3 | – |
| Essex | 17 | 792.3 | 301 | 1701 | 78 | 21.80 | 35.77 | 1.64 | 4 | 1 |
| Glamorgan | 11 | 423.1 | 185 | 873 | 54 | 16.16 | 34.38 | 2.12 | 5 | 1 |
| Gloucestershire | 19 | 799.1 | 360 | 1345 | 94 | 14.30 | 28.05 | 1.96 | 7 | 1 |
| Hampshire | 16 | 763.5 | 369 | 1262 | 72 | 17.52 | 27.53 | 1.57 | 4 | 1 |
| Kent | 16 | 625.2 | 264 | 1241 | 81 | 15.44 | 33.07 | 2.15 | 8 | 4 |
| Lancashire | 21 | 976.4 | 371 | 2014 | 99 | 20.34 | 34.36 | 1.68 | 6 | 3 |
| Leicestershire | 16 | 792.3 | 315 | 1618 | 87 | 18.59 | 34.02 | 1.82 | 6 | 1 |
| Middlesex | 19 | 797 | 357 | 1414 | 72 | 19.63 | 29.56 | 1.50 | 6 | 1 |
| Northamptonshire | 13 | 496.1 | 175 | 1028 | 52 | 19.76 | 34.53 | 1.74 | 2 | – |
| Nottinghamshire | 18 | 785.2 | 308 | 1578 | 74 | 21.32 | 33.48 | 1.57 | 4 | – |
| Somerset | 17 | 611.1 | 253 | 1139 | 87 | 13.09 | 31.06 | 2.37 | 9 | 3 |
| Surrey | 20 | 836.2 | 312 | 1750 | 103 | 16.99 | 34.87 | 2.05 | 8 | 1 |
| Sussex | 15 | 664.3 | 282 | 1244 | 87 | 14.29 | 31.20 | 2.18 | 9 | 2 |
| Warwickshire | 19 | 788 | 349 | 1515 | 80 | 18.08 | 32.04 | 1.69 | 5 | – |
| Worcestershire | 16 | 886.1 | 350 | 1675 | 102 | 16.43 | 31.50 | 1.91 | 9 | 3 |
| Totals | 271 | 11826.4 | 4910 | 22797 | 1280 | 17.81 | 32.12 | 1.80 | 95 | 22 |

Statistical Appendices                 161

## FOR YORKSHIRE – OTHER MATCHES
### BOWLING

| Yorkshire versus | M. | Overs | Mdns. | Runs | Wkts. | Avge. | Runs Per 100 Balls | Wkts. Per 100 Balls | 5 Wkts in an Inns | 10 Wkts in a Match |
|---|---|---|---|---|---|---|---|---|---|---|
| Australians | 6 | 215.2 | 69 | 470 | 20 | 23.50 | 36.37 | 1.54 | 2 | – |
| Cambridge University | 6 | 192 | 78 | 397 | 13 | 30.53 | 34.46 | 1.12 | 1 | – |
| Canadians | 1 | 24 | 8 | 59 | 5 | 11.80 | 40.97 | 3.47 | – | – |
| Gentlemen of Ireland | 1 | 48.2 | 20 | 78 | 6 | 13.00 | 26.89 | 2.06 | – | – |
| Indians | 1 | 28 | 14 | 69 | 0 | – | 41.07 | – | – | – |
| MCC | 20 | 739 | 233 | 1885 | 90 | 20.94 | 42.51 | 2.02 | 9 | 2 |
| New Zealanders | 3 | 134.5 | 43 | 334 | 12 | 27.83 | 41.28 | 1.48 | 2 | 1 |
| Oxford University | 9 | 325 | 128 | 659 | 47 | 14.02 | 33.79 | 2.41 | 5 | – |
| Pakistanis | 1 | 81.4 | 30 | 164 | 6 | 27.33 | 33.46 | 1.22 | – | – |
| Scotland | 4 | 191.1 | 91 | 325 | 20 | 16.25 | 28.33 | 1.74 | 1 | – |
| South Africans | 4 | 198.3 | 73 | 425 | 23 | 18.47 | 35.68 | 1.93 | 1 | – |
| West Indians | 3 | 142 | 59 | 255 | 17 | 15.00 | 29.92 | 1.99 | 1 | – |
| Totals | 59 | 2319.5 | 846 | 5120 | 259 | 19.76 | 36.78 | 1.86 | 22 | 3 |
| All Matches for Yorkshire | 330 | 14146.3 | 5756 | 27917 | 1539 | 18.13 | 32.89 | 1.83 | 117 | 25 |

## SUMMARY
### BOWLING

| | M. | Overs | Mdns. | Runs | Wkts. | Avge. | Runs Per 100 Balls | Wkts. Per 100 Balls | 5 Wkts in an Inns | 10 Wkts in a Match |
|---|---|---|---|---|---|---|---|---|---|---|
| For England | 28 | 210.4†<br>818.5 | 403 | 2080 | 102 | 20.39 | 31.52 | 1.54 | 5 | 1 |
| For Yorkshire | 330 | 14146.3 | 5756 | 27917 | 1539 | 18.13 | 32.89 | 1.83 | 117 | 25 |
| For other teams | 54 | 439.6†<br>1270.5 | 447 | 5030 | 205 | 24.53 | 45.14 | 1.83 | 12 | 3 |
| Totals | 412 | 650.2†<br>16236.1 | 6606 | 35027 | 1846 | 18.97 | 34.13 | 1.79 | 134 | 29 |

†8 ball overs

## GROUNDS IN YORKSHIRE
### BOWLING

| Ground | M. | Overs | Mdns. | Runs | Wkts. | Avge. | Runs Per 100 Balls | Wkts. Per 100 Balls | 5 Wkts in an Inns | 10 Wkts in a Match |
|---|---|---|---|---|---|---|---|---|---|---|
| Bradford | 36 | 1560.5 | 674 | 2942 | 162 | 18.16 | 31.41 | 1.72 | 12 | 1 |
| Harrogate | 9 | 392.4 | 164 | 763 | 45 | 16.95 | 32.38 | 1.91 | 2 | 1 |
| Huddersfield | 9 | 416.3 | 175 | 754 | 60 | 12.56 | 30.28 | 2.40 | 5 | 2 |
| Hull | 12 | 552.2 | 252 | 998 | 68 | 14.67 | 30.11 | 2.05 | 6 | 2 |
| Leeds | 31 | 1183 | 497 | 2281 | 121 | 18.85 | 32.13 | 1.70 | 9 | 3 |
| Middlesbrough | 2 | 20 | 12 | 22 | 0 | – | 18.33 | – | – | – |
| Scarborough | 41 | 1556.1 | 480 | 4295 | 153 | 28.07 | 45.99 | 1.63 | 8 | – |
| Sheffield | 43 | 1906.4 | 745 | 3833 | 210 | 18.25 | 33.50 | 1.83 | 18 | 2 |
| Totals | 183 | 7588.1 | 2999 | 15888 | 819 | 19.39 | 34.89 | 1.79 | 60 | 11 |

## SUMMARY
### BOWLING

| Grounds in | M. | Overs | Mdns. | Runs | Wkts. | Avge. | Runs Per 100 Balls | Wkts. Per 100 Balls | 5 Wkts. in an Inns | 10 Wkts. in a Match |
|---|---|---|---|---|---|---|---|---|---|---|
| UK | 368 | 15623.3 | 6262 | 31631 | 1671 | 18.92 | 33.74 | 1.78 | 122 | 25 |
| Australia | 14 | 269.7† | 61 | 832 | 37 | 22.48 | 38.53 | 1.71 | 2 | – |
| India | 1 | 34.4 | 4 | 117 | 4 | 29.25 | 56.25 | 1.92 | – | – |
| New Zealand | 4 | 165.4 | 74 | 334 | 20 | 16.70 | 33.60 | 2.01 | 1 | – |
| South Africa | 14 | 380.3† | 94 | 1103 | 90 | 12.25 | 36.24 | 2.95 | 8 | 4 |
| West Indies | 11 | 412.2 | 111 | 1010 | 24 | 42.08 | 40.82 | 0.97 | 1 | – |
| Total Overseas | 44 | 650.2†<br>612.4 | 344 | 3396 | 175 | 19.40 | 38.25 | 1.97 | 12 | 4 |
| Totals | 412 | 16236.1 | 6606 | 35027 | 1846 | 18.97 | 34.13 | 1.79 | 134 | 29 |

†8 ball overs

### CENTURY PARTNERSHIPS (5)

For England (1)
105: 7th Wkt. JHW (66) and L. Hutton (205) v West Indies, Sabina Park, Kingston, 1953–4

For Yorkshire (3)
148: 6th Wkt. JHW (60) and N. W. D. Yardley (183*) v Hampshire at Leeds, 1951
109: 6th Wkt. JHW (79) and J. V. Wilson (64) v Lancashire at Manchester, 1951
132: 8th Wkt. JHW (65) and W. Watson (119) v Leicestershire at Leicester, 1949

For MCC (1)
112: 6th Wkt. JHW (63) and J. V. Wilson (62*) v Tasmania at Launceston, 1954–5

### FIFTIES (18)

For England (2)
66 v West Indies at Sabina Park, Kingston, 1953–4
54 v Pakistan at Manchester, 1954

For Yorkshire (15)
79 v Lancashire at Manchester 1951
74 v South Africans at Sheffield, 1955
72 v Pakistanis at Sheffield, 1954
70 v Worcestershire at Sheffield, 1949
66* v Sussex at Hull, 1954
65 v Leicestershire at Leicester, 1949
64 v West Indians at Sheffield, 1957
63* v Gentlemen of Ireland at Harrogate, 1947
60 v Hampshire at Leeds, 1951
59* v Somerset at Taunton, 1950
55* v Warwickshire at Bradford, 1956
54 v Surrey at Sheffield, 1954
52* v Gloucestershire at Bristol, 1950
51 v Northamptonshire at Northampton, 1947
50 v Kent at Leeds, 1952

For MCC (1)
63 v Tasmania at Launceston, 1954–5

## RUNS IN BOUNDARIES – FOR YORKSHIRE

| Season | Runs for Yorkshire | 6's | 4's | Runs in Boundaries | % of Total |
|---|---|---|---|---|---|
| 1946 | 12 | – | 1 | 4 | 33.33 |
| 1947 | 581 | 12 | 60 | 312 | 53.70 |
| 1948 | 412 | 9 | 48 | 246 | 59.70 |
| 1949 | 412 | 5 | 55 | 250 | 60.67 |
| 1950 | 679 | 13 | 84 | 414 | 60.97 |
| 1951 | 559 | 15 | 61 | 334 | 59.74 |
| 1952 | 620 | 17 | 73 | 394 | 63.54 |
| 1953 | 423 | 13 | 36 | 222 | 52.48 |
| 1954 | 397 | 11 | 41 | 230 | 57.93 |
| 1955 | 368 | 18 | 35 | 248 | 67.39 |
| 1956 | 480 | 11 | 57 | 294 | 61.25 |
| 1957 | 519 | 14 | 57 | 312 | 60.11 |
| 1958 | 303 | 9 | 36 | 198 | 65.34 |
| Totals | 5765 | 147 | 644 | 3458 | 59.98 |

## HOW OUT
### (ALL FIRST-CLASS MATCHES)

| | | |
|---|---|---|
| Caught | 236 | 51.98% |
| Bowled | 150 | 33.04% |
| Leg Before Wicket | 37 | 8.15% |
| Stumped | 23 | 5.07% |
| Run Out | 8 | 1.76% |
| Totals | 454 | 100.00% |

### SIXTEEN WICKETS IN A MATCH (1)
For Yorkshire
16 for 112 (9 for 48 and 7 for 64) v Sussex at Hull, 1954

### FOURTEEN WICKETS IN A MATCH (1)
For MCC
14 for 96 (6 for 16 and 8 for 80) v Orange Free State at Bloemfontein, 1956–7

### TWELVE WICKETS IN A MATCH (5)
For England (1)
12 for 89 (5 for 53 and 7 for 36) v South Africa at Cape Town, 1956–7
For Yorkshire (4)
12 for 85 (9 for 25 and 3 for 60) v Lancashire at Manchester, 1954
12 for 90 (4 for 64 and 8 for 26) v Middlesex at Lord's, 1950
12 for 122 (5 for 81 and 7 for 41) v Surrey at The Oval, 1949
12 for 160 (7 for 88 and 5 for 72) v Essex at Westcliff-on-Sea, 1948

## ELEVEN WICKETS IN A MATCH (9)

For Yorkshire (9)
11 for 48 (6 for 25 and 5 for 23) v MCC at Lord's, 1953
11 for 58 (6 for 21 and 5 for 37) v Glamorgan at Leeds, 1951
11 for 70 (7 for 34 and 4 for 36) v Somerset at Leeds, 1957
11 for 98 (5 for 69 and 6 for 29) v Kent at Canterbury, 1952
11 for 123 (6 for 57 and 5 for 66) v Hampshire at Hull, 1949
11 for 128 (4 for 54 and 7 for 74) v Leicestershire at Leicester, 1953
11 for 136 (4 for 64 and 7 for 72) v Worcestershire at Worcester, 1955
11 for 147 (7 for 56 and 4 for 91) v Worcestershire at Huddersfield, 1953
11 for 176 (5 for 92 and 6 for 84) v New Zealanders at Sheffield, 1949

## NINE WICKETS IN AN INNINGS (2)

For Yorkshire (2)
9 for 25 v Lancashire at Manchester, 1954
9 for 48 v Sussex at Hull, 1954 (1st Innings)

## EIGHT WICKETS IN AN INNINGS (3)

For Yorkshire (2)
8 for 26 v Middlesex at Lord's, 1950
8 for 87 v Derbyshire at Chesterfield, 1948
For MCC (1)
8 for 80 v Orange Free State at Bloemfontein, 1956–7

## SEVEN WICKETS IN AN INNINGS (14)

For England (2)
7 for 36 v South Africa at Cape Town, 1956–7
7 for 56 v Pakistan at The Oval, 1954
For Yorkshire (11)
7 for 34 v Somerset at Leeds, 1957
7 for 41 v Surrey at The Oval, 1949
7 for 49 v Middlesex at Sheffield, 1952
7 for 56 v Worcestershire at Huddersfield, 1953
7 for 64 v Sussex at Hull, 1954 (2nd Innings)
7 for 65 v Worcestershire at Worcester, 1950
7 for 66 v Middlesex at Leeds, 1947
7 for 72 v Worcestershire at Worcester, 1955
7 for 74 v Leicestershire at Leicester, 1953
7 for 88 v Essex at Westcliff-on-Sea, 1948
7 for 119 v Surrey at Leeds, 1952

For MCC (1)
7 for 20 v Griqualand West at Kimberley, 1956–7

## HOW THE WICKETS WERE TAKEN
### (ALL FIRST CLASS MATCHES)

| | | |
|---|---|---|
| Caught | 960 | 52.00% |
| Bowled | 531 | 28.77% |
| Leg Before Wicket | 238 | 12.89% |
| Stumped | 112 | 6.07% |
| Hit Wicket | 5 | 0.27% |
| Totals | 1846 | 100.00% |

## G. A. R. LOCK
## IN FIRST-CLASS CRICKET 1946-58
### BOWLING

| Season | M. | Overs | Mdns. | Runs | Wkts. | Avge. | Runs Per 100 Balls | Wkts. Per 100 Balls | 5 Wkts. in an Inns | 10 Wkts. in a Match |
|---|---|---|---|---|---|---|---|---|---|---|
| 1946 | 1 | 10 | 2 | 24 | 0 | – | 40.00 | – | – | – |
| 1947 | 2 | 56 | 15 | 128 | 4 | 32.00 | 38.09 | 1.19 | – | – |
| 1948 | 2 | 64 | 12 | 168 | 11 | 15.27 | 43.75 | 2.86 | 2 | – |
| 1949 | 25 | 754.5 | 287 | 1672 | 67 | 24.95 | 36.91 | 1.47 | – | – |
| 1950 | 26 | 921.2 | 372 | 1762 | 74 | 23.81 | 31.87 | 1.33 | 3 | – |
| 1951 | 32 | 1155.4 | 448 | 2237 | 105 | 21.30 | 32.26 | 1.51 | 5 | – |
| 1952 | 32 | 1109.4 | 416 | 2237 | 131 | 17.07 | 33.59 | 1.96 | 6 | 1 |
| 1953 | 19 | 732.1 | 282 | 1590 | 100 | 15.90 | 36.19 | 2.27 | 8 | 2 |
| 1953–4 (West Indies) | 9 | 486.1 | 157 | 1178 | 28 | 42.07 | 40.38 | 0.95 | 1 | – |
| 1954 | 32 | 1027.1 | 411 | 2000 | 125 | 16.00 | 32.45 | 2.02 | 7 | 2 |
| 1955 | 33 | 1407.4 | 497 | 3109 | 216 | 14.39 | 36.81 | 2.55 | 18 | 6 |
| 1955–6 (Pakistan) | 11 | 557 | 296 | 869 | 81 | 10.72 | 26.00 | 2.42 | 10 | 4 |
| 1956 | 26 | 1058.2 | 437 | 1932 | 155 | 12.46 | 30.42 | 2.44 | 15 | 5 |
| 1956–7 (South Africa) | 14 | 352.7† | 120 | 833 | 56 | 14.87 | 29.50 | 1.98 | 4 | 2 |
| 1957 | 31 | 1194.1 | 449 | 2550 | 212 | 12.02 | 35.58 | 2.95 | 21 | 9 |
| 1958 | 29 | 1014.4 | 382 | 2055 | 170 | 12.08 | 33.75 | 2.79 | 14 | 3 |
| Totals | 324 | 352.7†<br>11548.5 | 4583 | 24344 | 1535 | 15.85 | 33.75 | 2.12 | 114 | 34 |

†8 ball overs

### TEST MATCHES
### (1952–8)
### BOWLING

| Season | M. | Overs | Mdns. | Runs | Wkts. | Avge. | Runs Per 100 Balls | Wkts. Per 100 Balls | 5 Wkts. in an Inns | 10 Wkts. in a Match |
|---|---|---|---|---|---|---|---|---|---|---|
| 1952 v India | 2 | 15.3 | 7 | 37 | 4 | 9.25 | 39.78 | 4.30 | – | – |
| 1953 v Australia | 2 | 61 | 21 | 165 | 8 | 20.68 | 45.08 | 2.18 | 1 | – |
| 1953–4 v West Indies | 5 | 292.5 | 87 | 718 | 14 | 51.28 | 40.85 | 0.79 | – | – |
| 1955 v South Africa | 3 | 164 | 65 | 353 | 13 | 27.15 | 35.87 | 1.32 | – | – |
| 1956 v Australia | 4 | 237.2 | 115 | 337 | 15 | 22.46 | 23.66 | 1.05 | – | – |
| 1956–7 v South Africa | 1 | 26† | 11 | 38 | 2 | 19.00 | 18.26 | 0.96 | – | – |
| 1957 v West Indies | 3 | 114.2 | 59 | 163 | 15 | 10.86 | 23.76 | 2.18 | 2 | 1 |
| 1958 v New Zealand | 5 | 176 | 93 | 254 | 34 | 7.47 | 24.05 | 3.21 | 3 | 1 |
| Totals | 25 | 26†<br>1061 | 458 | 2065 | 105 | 19.66 | 31.41 | 1.59 | 6 | 2 |

†8 ball overs

## SLOW LEFT-ARM BOWLERS – A TEST COMPARISON

| Player | Tests | Balls | Runs | Wkts. | Avge. | Runs Per 100 Balls | Wkts. Per 100 Balls |
|---|---|---|---|---|---|---|---|
| R. Peel | 20 | 5216 | 1715 | 102 | 16.81 | 32.87 | 1.95 |
| W. Rhodes | 58 | 8231 | 3425 | 127 | 26.96 | 41.61 | 1.54 |
| H. Verity | 40 | 11173 | 3510 | 144 | 24.37 | 31.41 | 1.28 |
| J. H. Wardle | 28 | 6597 | 2080 | 102 | 20.39 | 31.52 | 1.54 |
| G. A. R. Lock | 49 | 13147 | 4451 | 174 | 25.58 | 33.85 | 1.32 |
| D. L. Underwood | 86 | 21862 | 7674 | 297 | 25.83 | 35.10 | 1.35 |

# Index

(Compiled by L. F. Hancock)

Adcock, N. A. T., 88, 90, 101
Aird, R., 115
Allen, G., 19
Allen, M. H. J., 63
Allen, Sir George, 59, 77–8, 143–4
Alley, W. E., 123
Amarnath, N. B., 127
Ames, L. E. G., 59
Andrew, K. V., 58, 63–4, 98, 107
Appleyard, R., 28, 34, 39, 41–50, 63–4, 83–8, 105–6, 109–10, 113–14, 120, 141, 154
Archer, R. G., 75
Arlott, J., 57, 74–5, 79, 87
Ashman, J. R., 33

Bailey, T. E., 38, 53, 63–4, 76, 81, 83, 90, 96–102, 141–2
Bannister, A., 56, 59, 80
Barber, W., 29, 32
Barlow, E. J., 125, 135
Barnes, S. F., 42, 91, 128
Barton, M. R., 146
Bateson, K., 18
Bedser, A. V., 40, 43, 50, 75–6, 78, 83–4
Benaud, R., 76, 87
Berry, R., 58–9, 78
Binks, J. G., 142
Birkenshaw, J., 117
Bolus, J. B., 150
Booth, A., 29–31
Booth, R., 39
Botham, I. T., 139
Bowes, W. E., 26–7, 31–2, 38–9, 42, 45–8, 58, 73, 88, 108, 144, 156
Bradman, Sir Donald, 36–7
Brearley, J. M., 149–51
Brennan, D. V., 30
Brown, F. R., 31, 58, 101
Brown, W. A., 37
Buckley, Major F., 15, 145
Burnet, J. R., 105, 107–8, 111, 114–21, 123
Butcher, B. F., 125, 135

Cardus, Sir Neville, 56, 62
Cave, H. B., 61
Cheetham, J. E., 88
Chester, F., 143
Chew, J., 133–4
Clarke, J., 131, 134
Close, D. B., 34–5, 40, 45, 107–11, 119, 140
Compton, D. C. S., 26, 32, 78, 81–4
Constantine, Lord, 123, 127
Cook, W., 124
Cope, G. A., 111–12, 139, 142–3, 148–51, 154–5
Copson, W. H., 29
Cowan, M. J., 51, 110–11, 118–19, 148, 157
Cowdrey, M. C., 58, 61, 86, 96, 102
Coxon, A., 29, 146
Crook, M., 15
Crouch, M., 135, 136

Davidson, A. K., 75
Davidson, K. R., 30
De Courcy, J. H., 75
Dexter, E. R., 61
Douglas, J. W. H. T., 92
Duerr, F., 124
Duffus, L., 91

Eddleston, M., 131
Edrich, W. J., 31, 78, 137
Ellis, F., 16
Ellis, S., 15
Emanuel, G., 157
Endean, W. R., 90, 93, 95–6, 102–3
Evans, T. G., 30, 56, 60, 62, 64, 75, 78, 81, 84, 87, 96–7, 141, 145, 147

Farnell, D., 136
Fazal Mahmood, 82, 84
Fielden, S., 155–6
Flatley, K., 134
Fleetwood-Smith, L. O'B., 96
Fletcher, D. G. W., 45, 50–1
Fortune, C., 91, 98
Fry, C. B., 54

Funston, K. J., 99, 101–4

Gilchrist, R., 127
Gillhouley, K., 136
Gladwin, C., 29, 40
Goddard, J. D. C., 79
Goddard, T. L., 89, 95–6, 102
Grace, Dr W. G., 98
Graveney, T. W., 56, 80–1, 84, 88
Grieves, K. J., 35, 132
Griffith, S. C., 78
Griffith, C. C., 125, 127, 132–4
Gupte, S. P., 128

Haigh, A., 125–6
Hall, W. W., 125, 130
Hamer, A., 118
Hammond, W. R., 96
Hardstaff, J. (Jnr), 78
Harris, Lord, 55
Hartley, K., 122, 127
Harvey, R. N., 75, 86
Hassett, A. L., 75
Hawke, N. J. M., 125, 130
Headley, G. A., 59
Heaton, C., 17
Heine, P. S., 90, 96
Hesketh, C., 113, 120
Hilton, M. J., 78
Hirst, G. H., 17
Hole, G. B., 75–6
Hollies, W. E., 79
Holt, J. K., 80
Howard, N. D., 35, 110
Howorth, R., 29, 78
Howson, C., 20
Humphries, J., 18–19
Hurst, B., 128–35
Hutton, Sir Leonard, 27, 29, 32, 48–9, 59–60, 75–8, 81–2, 84–8, 96

Ikin, J. T., 78
Illingworth, R., 27, 44–5, 109–10, 118–19
Insole, D. J., 57–8, 92, 94, 97, 100, 102

# Index

Jackson, P. F., 29
Jardine, D. R., 85
Jenkins, R. O., 78
Johnson, I. W., 60, 87
Johnston, W. A., 85–7

Kay, J., 125
Keighley, W. G., 146
Keith, H. J., 89, 95, 102
Kilburn, J. M., 30, 32, 36, 38, 41, 46, 83, 89, 140
Kilner, C., 16

Laker, J. C., 26, 43, 48, 50–2, 56–61, 63, 74–7, 81–2, 84, 90, 96, 98–9, 102–6, 139, 143, 154
Lancaster, T., 124
Langridge, J. G., 46
Larwood, H., 85
Lee, C., 16, 33, 113–14, 118
Lenham, L. J., 44
Lester, E. I., 28, 33–4, 57, 117, 143, 146
Leyland, M., 26, 29, 32, 156
Lillee, D. K., 62
Lilley, W., 17
Lindwall, R. R., 75, 86, 122, 127, 143
Loader, P. J., 50–1, 100
Lock, H. C., 56
Lock, G. A. R., 39, 49–64, 73–85, 88–90, 94, 99–102, 125, 154
Lomas, D., 128, 130–1
Lowson, F. A., 44, 89, 106, 113, 120

McCarthy, C. N., 55
McConnon, J., 83–4
McDonald, E. A., 127
McGlew, D. J., 88–9, 95
McIntyre, A. J. W., 50, 61
McLean, R. A., 89, 97–8, 102–3
McWatt, C. A., 80, 82
Maddocks, L. V., 87
Manning, J. S., 63
Marlar, R. G., 141
Marsden, J., 124, 128
Mason, A., 30, 33, 37
May, P. B. H., 28, 45, 48, 50–1, 53, 55, 62, 80, 84, 86, 88, 94–6, 100–5, 115, 144
Meckiff, I., 73
Merritt, W. E., 128
Millard, P., 74–5
Miller, K. R., 75–6, 87, 144
Mitchell, A., 42
Morris, A. R., 75, 85–6
Muncer, B. L., 36

Nash, J. H., 106, 120
Newstead, J. T., 128
Nourse, A. D., 92

Nurse, S. M., 125, 135

O'Reilly, W. J., 42

Padgett, D. E. V., 119
Pardon, C. F., 54–5
Peebles, I. A. R., 84, 86, 88, 141
Peel, R., 54
Pegg, C., 18
Percival, K., 153
Pettiford, J., 110
Platt, R. K., 19, 44–5, 63, 109, 112, 115, 117–18
Pollard, A., 124
Pope, G. H., 29
Porter, G., 18
Preston, N., 55
Price, W. F. F., 55
Pritchard, T. L., 36

Ramadhin, S., 60, 80–1
Rhodes, W., 28, 30, 36, 38, 42, 77, 79
Richards, I. V. A., 128, 154
Richardson, P. E., 100–1
Robertson, J. D. B., 38, 78
Robertson Glasgow, R. C., 145
Robins, R. W. V., 32
Robinson, A. L., 150
Robinson, Basil, 112–13
Robinson, Ellis, 17, 18, 30, 114
Robinson, Emmott, 44, 46
Rorke, G. F., 73
Ross, A., 94, 103
Rowan, A. M. B., 96
Ryan, M., 117

Sellers, A. B., 23, 31–3, 42, 49, 107, 156
Shakespeare, W., 129
Sharpe, P. J., 117, 120
Shaw, A., 49
Simpson, R. B., 123, 125
Simpson, R. T., 39
Sims, J. M., 38
Smailes, T. F., 29–30
Smedley, M. J., 136
Smith, D. (Nelson), 126
Smith, D. (Rishton), 131
Smith, G. O., 123, 126
Smith, J. (Rishton), 134
Smith, V. I., 141
Smithson, G. A., 30
Sobers, Sir Garfield, 59–60, 82
Spooner, R. T., 60
Statham, J. B., 76, 85–7, 89, 100, 102
Stead, B., 136
Stollmeyer, J. B., 79
Stott, W. B., 117
Surridge, W. S., 32, 48–9, 56
Sutcliffe, H., 14, 32, 48

Sutcliffe, W. H. H., 34–5, 44, 48, 50, 64, 108–9, 114
Swanton, E. W., 26, 30, 43, 59, 61, 63, 78–80, 82, 86, 92, 100–1, 107, 139

Tattersall, R., 58, 79, 140
Tayfield, H. J., 88–90, 94, 96, 98–102, 104, 141
Taylor, B., 97–8
Taylor, H. W., 91–2
Taylor, K., 117
Thomson, A. A., 140
Titmus, F. J., 88
Tribe, G. E., 26, 49, 63–4, 98
Trueman, F. S., 28, 39, 41–2, 47–8, 50–1, 82, 88, 110, 115, 120, 143
Turner, C., 30, 108
Tyson, F. H., 47–8, 57, 85–8, 98, 144

Valentine, A. L., 80, 124
Van Ryneveld, C. B., 93
Verity, H., 28–30, 36, 38, 79, 85, 123
Voce, W., 85
Vogler, A. E. E., 128

Waite, J. H. B., 89, 96
Walcott, C. L., 78, 82
Walcott, H., 59–60
Walsh, J. E., 26, 36
Walters, H., 13, 15, 17
Wardle, Jack (Father), 13
Wardle, Jane (Mother), 13
Wardle, Edna, (Mrs Wardle), 20–3, 92, 106, 112, 115, 151–3, 155–7
Wardle, Gerald (Son), 23–5
Wardle, John (Son), 22–5
Warner, Sir Pelham, 78
Washbrook, C., 73, 78, 146
Watkins, J. C., 96–7
Watson, W., 29, 50–1, 80–1, 106
Weekes, E. de C., 78, 123
Welsh, T., 125
Wharton, A., 46, 146
White, J. C., 31
Wilson, D., 117, 142
Wilson, J. V., 50, 57, 116
Winslow, P. L., 88–9
Wood, N., 123, 126
Wood, R., 33
Worrell, Sir Frank, 78, 81
Wright, D. V. P., 78, 97

Yardley, N. W. D., 28, 33, 36–7, 39, 41–5, 59, 64, 73, 112
Young, J. A., 40